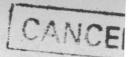

THAT
SUMMER

First published in 2004 by
Virgin Books
Thames Wharf Studios
Rainville Rd
London W6 9HA

Published under licence by Independent News and Media (UK) Ltd

ISBN 0 7535 0884 2

Typeset by TW Typesetiing, Plymouth, Devon
Printed and bound by Mackays of Chatham PLC

CONTENTS

1980s

1990s and beyond

INTRODUCTION BY SIMON CALDER

Joy and anger, triumph and disaster, passion and tears – a typical day on the travel desk of the *Independent*, perhaps, but also the range of emotions that going on holiday can generate. Travel memories have a habit of transforming over time, so that the lashing rain and striking air-traffic controllers that blighted your trip to Greece are quickly forgotten in favour of the more comfortable, selective recollections of warm afternoons, cool seas and cold beers. But on journeys that change us, the mental snapshots and soundbites prove strangely vivid and robust even many summers later. Each of us has experienced a summer that was wilder, more intense, more passionate than any other: the holiday when the world came to life – and changed our lives.

The smell of bread baking, garlic roasting or grapes fermenting can trigger instant recall of a first summer abroad. A line from a song that was a summer hit that year could steer you straight back to the moment when you first tasted freedom and/or another traveller's lips, and the strong sense of place that the memories evoke.

This is a book about journeys that, on one level, are about the business of getting from A to B – which should have been a simple matter but, for some of our writers, proved incredibly difficult. Yet they are also about something far more profound. These are voyages of discovery for the soul. Only by leaving the familiar environment of home and taking your chances on the road do you find hidden strengths in yourself, or expose weaknesses in a relationship. Once you escape from the small domains in which most of us dwell, the scale and spectrum of the world can terrify and transform you.

Some say that life is not complete until you have stood in the rain outside Lyon or Stuttgart for twelve hours failing to hitch a lift, and been arrested for offending the national flag or morals of at least two countries. Well, it worked for me. But this book shows that acting as a low-rent nomad is just one of many routes to enlightenment, with detours to confusion and dismay thrown in. The 54 fine summers you are about to read are full of revelations in every sense: errors of judgement and navigation, loves found and lost, and a sprinkling (or should that be an inhalation?) of illicit substances. To help place them in context, I have added a line about significant travel events of the summer in question. 'The past is foreign country', wrote LP Hartley in *The Go-Between*. 'They do things differently there.'

The man who realised the potential of this far-off land, and who unlocked the wealth of travel memories it concealed, was Stephen Wood – then Weekend Editor of the *Independent*, now Executive Editor of Condé Nast *Traveller*. From the time of its first season in the summer of 1994, That Summer has been remarkably self-sustaining series: each story has triggered other writers to describe their formative holiday. I have picked the best of the decade, and – to strengthen this collection still further – commissioned previously unpublished stories from people with passionate tales about the journey from adolescence into adulthood, via independence and liberation. In ten years on the travel desk at the *Independent*, I have learned three pieces of fortune-cookie philosophy, which I would like to share with you:

1. Life is a journey, and vice-versa.
2. For every negative travel event, there is an equal and opposite positive one.
3. In that box of old, blurred and curled holiday snaps that you haven't looked at for years, the person you do not recognise – and who is wearing ridiculous clothes, hair and expression – is quite probably you.

Simon Calder is one of Britain's best-known travel experts. He is travel editor of the *Independent* newspaper and reports for the BBC's *Holiday* programme.

1950s and 1960s

CUSTOMS AND EXERCISE, 1951

In 1951 Elizabeth Candlish cycled across the borders of post-war paranoia in Europe.

Spending the night in the customs post between Holland and Germany wasn't part of the plan. We meant to cross the border, and perhaps find the youth hostel in Aachen. But it turned out that the hostel was being rebuilt. Besides, we were two very wet and bedraggled British teenagers, and the customs men were perhaps just a little bored that day in the summer of 1951.

My friend Margaret had a German pen pal in Heidelberg, so to Heidelberg we would go, cycling. We took a tent (neither of us had camped before) and home-made sleeping bags. From our homes in St Andrews, Fife, we caught a train to London, and from there took a coach to Dover where we retrieved the bikes that we'd sent on ahead of us. As we pedalled our way off the boat at Ostend it was a daunting thought that we'd never cycled further than twenty miles at a stretch.

By the time we reached that frontier post we'd been six days on the road, often in rain. Campsites as we know them now had not yet been invented, and we'd camped on small Belgian farms, twice sleeping snugly in a barn. We'd been invited into spotless farm kitchens and had met whole families, usually three generations, speaking a dialect that our schoolgirl French and German could not decipher, but somehow we communicated.

The French told us about the war and about the liberation, and they wanted to ask about Britain – why were we still rationed? Why had the British voted Churchill out of office – he won the war, didn't he? Everywhere our wet things were taken off to be dried and cans of hot water produced: payment was firmly refused. In the mornings we'd be waved off, with pressing invitations to come again on our return journey.

Our route took us briefly into the Netherlands, to visit friends in Maastricht, then we headed for the German border. Back home, some people had warned us against going into Germany. After all, the war was not so far in the past. Margaret's uncle was a detective at Scotland Yard: if in trouble, he said, we were to go to the military police – and of course he himself could be contacted at Whitehall 1212.

We reached Vaals, at the Dutch–German frontier, before 4 p.m., once again wet and rather miserable. As usual, there were two barriers, and two sets of offices to go through, and our passports were stamped in both. We were leaving Holland, so we were not of much interest to the Dutch. But we were entering Germany, and the inspector of immigrants wanted to know our plans. Camping? In this weather? Better to make for the youth hostel in Aachen – he would telephone to book us a place. And that was how we heard that it was being rebuilt – the war, you know.

The inspector made up his mind to befriend us. There was a hostel in Vaals, a Dutch hostel: we could go there. And he had another suggestion: we should send our bicycles ahead by rail to Cologne, and next day he would arrange a lift for us. It was no problem to find lifts at the frontier. Why, only that day three Australian girls got one for a hundred miles.

My letter home takes up the story: 'Well, it was an awful day, and this seemed ideal. We cycled into Aachen, found the station, and sent off the bikes. Our friend the inspector turned up and helped us fill in the forms, which were a bit complicated. We sent our saddlebags too, taking out only a few belongings, and tying these in a bundle. We must have looked like displaced persons. Then the inspector took us back to the frontier by tram, and we put on dry socks and shoes in his office, and he took us for coffee, and got the waiter to add something to it: it tasted awful, but it certainly warmed us up. Then we found out that we were too late to get into the youth hostel so the inspector said that he would find us somewhere to sleep at the frontier station, and meanwhile he would take us out to supper.

'He took us to a restaurant in Vaals, and we each got a huge plate of two fried eggs, bacon, bread, tomatoes, gherkin and goodness knows what else besides. It was marvellous. Later he and another customs officer took us for coffee, and told us their war stories and adventures . . . Then we went back to the customs post. There was a little room there where night-duty men sometimes slept – only one camp bed, but they spread heavy packages of forms on the floor, and left us their coats. We tossed for the bed, and I lost! I can't say we got much sleep – there was traffic all through the night, and voices and footsteps.

'We got up about half-past six, washed, tied up our bundles, and sat outside in very pale sunshine, having breakfast. About half-past eight a customs man rushed out, and said, "Quick – here's a bus going to Cologne." He picked up our bundles and threw them into the bus, and we got in and off we went.'

We were, we discovered, the guests of a Dutch insurance firm from Echt on their annual outing. They would stop at Cologne on their homeward way. Meanwhile they were happy to have us along, and to take us with them up into the mountains. Before we left them in the evening we had promised to include Echt on our route back and see them again. And we did.

So we reached Cologne on the day we'd planned, but not until 8 p.m. – and eventually found a bed (illegally) in the Toc H Club. And we reached Heidelberg, too. In the Rhine valley there was no place to pitch a tent, and we joined the German youth hostel movement. Some of the hostels were centuries-old buildings, and one or two had been purpose-built for the Hitler Youth Movement, but none provided us with a lodging quite as strange as the one we had that night on the border at Vaals.

On 4 May 1951, the 'Dome of Discovery' opened on London's South Bank, at the start of the Festival of Britain.

OCEAN LINER TO A BRAVE, NEWLYWED WORLD, 1953

Peter Rich recalls the week when he got married and embarked on a great liner for a New York honeymoon and life in Canada.

Summer 1953. The plan is activated. Sunday: get married. Monday: sail to the New World on a great ocean liner. The Monday after: honeymoon in New York, followed by a new life in Canada.

Well, it worked out; but the strain of a traditional wedding, the trauma of departure and the excitement of the voyage were a severe test for the new partnership of two 23-year-old optimists.

Europe in the early 1950s was another world. The old, rigid orders and establishments were in place and unashamedly flaunted, although cracks were visible. The 'dos' and 'don'ts' of family life, and the rituals of each sector of society were, in the main, intact. In Britain, austerity and tradition were stifling; but for those of us with health, energy and a British passport there was a range of countries that wanted us.

The months of anguish planning the combined wedding and farewell party paid off, and the day went well. Tears flowed, advice was showered upon us. Rich Uncle Joe advised us to travel first class. Uncle Sam, an ex-ship's musician, suggested that by a careful reading of the ship's fire-escape diagrams we should find our way to the first-class bar and lounge.

Conforming to tradition, we spent our wedding night in a luxury West End hotel. Amid the Art-Deco splendour of the

Strand Palace we sat cross-legged on a giant double bed surrounded by torn-open envelopes, notes of congratulation and lots of paper money. Three changes of clothes had resulted in 21 pockets and two handbags continuously and discreetly fed to overflowing with gifts of money, for it was known that we could not take any bulky presents.

Early on Monday we went to the parental homes for the last, terrible, emigrants' goodbyes. The old guilt still nags, the scene slips into focus as it has done repeatedly over the years: Mother almost fainting, believing that she would never see us again; support from Sister, saying 'go, go'; Father in the background, silent, hands saying 'go', eyes saying 'stay'.

The boat train was an event in itself: excitement, smart people with smart luggage, steam, kisses, tears, waves, hats, veils, leather handbags and gloves, fur coats, more steam, porters, whistles. Alfred Hitchcock, boarding the train with his double bass, would have gone unnoticed. We sat holding hands, trying to stay calm. We had been married for 22 hours.

The *Île de France* was the last and greatest of the French transatlantic liners. She started from Cherbourg and collected passengers in Southampton. She was too large to dock, so we were taken out in small boats. The sea was extremely rough, and we battled waves as we headed out to where the beautiful, 1930s-style, picture-book liner lay at anchor.

As our little bobbing boat was manoeuvred closer, we got an idea of the scale and solidity of the ship. Great waves crashed against a gigantic black-painted steel wall, which did not move. The seas broke around the ship as though it were solid land. (I was to remember this image when, in mid-Atlantic, we were hit by violent storms that tossed the liner about as though it were a little boat.)

Looking up, we could see tiny faces against the skyline some sixty feet above our heads. A steel door opened, a collapsible stair was lowered and we were helped aboard by polite French sailors. Stewards led us along softly lit carpeted corridors to our tiny (internal) Tourist Class cabin. Awaiting us were telegrams, flowers – and, taking up most of the floor space, our second-hand cabin trunk. By the time we reached Montreal it had cost more in porters' tips than we had originally paid for it.

The first part of our honeymoon was spent sleeping in one bunk of a two-bunk cabin. The ability to sleep with each other this way became a habit, and for many years visitors to our bedroom were puzzled by the single bed.

Exploring the gigantic ship we soon realised we were not aboard a floating hotel but something more complex – a complete microcosm of the pre-war and post-war European world. All the social hierarchies, together with their physical manifestations, were replicated. Three main classes: Tourist, Second and First, each with subdivisions to do with size, location and 'en suite facilities'.

Each sector was luxuriously furnished in an appropriate manner: cabins, table and bed linen, cutlery and uniforms – everything obeyed hierarchical rules. Maple in Tourist, oak in Second, and mahogany, ebony, chrome and glass in First. And the staff! From the imperious presence of the head waiter in the first-class dining-room down through an army of waiters, assistants, chefs, cooks, bakers, stewards, maids, nurses, musicians, valets, cabin boys and kennel maids. All these and many more, just to look after the passengers. Looking after the ship were two main groups of crew. Wherever their duties brought them into contact with passengers, smartly dressed bilingual officers and sailors formed a cast of extras supporting the star, a magnificent silver-haired and silver-bearded captain. Beyond and below, hordes of unseen crew, including dark-skinned sweating boilermen in the inferno of the ship's bowels, kept us moving steadily forward.

On one of our safaris into deepest shipland we wandered beyond the world of luxury into 'The Works'. The line between the two worlds was the thickness of a two-inch door. On one side were carpets, oak and brass, and the hum of ventilation systems. Over the threshold we entered what seemed to be a Sheffield steel factory. Metal plates lined the back of our entry door, the floors and walls. The whole place throbbed with the sound of machinery.

Directly opposite us was a large industrial lift, filled to capacity with bundles of laundry. In the distance we could see a huge, busy kitchen. Men in various work-clothes were attending the ship with a devotion equal to that shown to the passengers on the other side of the door.

In another part we looked down three or four storeys into a pit where men in white overalls wandered among machinery such as I had once seen in Battersea Power Station. I remember feeling a surge of almost mystical realisation: we were part of a species that had the ability and courage to conceive, build and run such an enterprise as an ocean-going liner; our potential must be limitless.

We soon settled to the daily routine. Breakfast with menus and newspapers printed on board, fresh croissants and baguettes from the bakery. By the fourth morning so many passengers and waiters had succumbed to seasickness that those of us remaining were placed on a single table in the corner of the huge dining room.

We spent the mornings in deckchairs, wrapped in thick blankets by stewards who pampered us and served hominy soup at 11 a.m. precisely. Deck games were quoits for us, clay-pigeon shooting for the other ranks of passengers. A five-course lunch, and a six-course dinner plus wines and liqueurs: we could rarely do justice to the quantity of excellent cuisine. Ship's officers organised afternoon games and tea dances in the ballroom. Evenings were for musical shows, fancy-dress balls, drinking at one of the bars or gentle gambling; deck horse-racing (wooden 'horses' were moved by stewards when their number came up) and a form of bingo in Tourist, roulette and chemin de fer in First.

We often slipped away from all these activities, and by a circuitous route 'went to the dogs'. The steadiest part of the ship was on the topmost deck between the funnels. Two runs of kennels faced each other across an expanse of empty deck. We would lie side by side looking up at dark clouds or starry sky, trying hard not to look at the horizon, which would slowly rise way above the ship's rail, reach its zenith, give an awful twist (a shudder ran the length of the ship), then sink out of sight before rising again. (We later discovered that seasickness can be avoided by looking only at the horizon.)

It is a tradition at sea to be invited to the Captain's Table. Of the hundreds of passengers, only a few could be selected. I think we were chosen because it was known we were on our honeymoon. One morning an elaborately printed invitation was slipped under our door. 'The captain would be honoured . . . in the First Class Dining Room . . . Dress: Formal.'

Out came the crumpled wedding clothes to be pressed and, by 8.30 p.m., we were sitting at table looking poised. I cannot now remember the other guests, only some of the conversation, which ranged up and down the table in French, English and Dutch. From horses and sporting guns (about which we were ignorant), the conversation turned to war experiences. Our stories of the London Blitz and of being child evacuees were swapped for those about life in enemy-occupied countries.

And then: New York harbour, the Statue of Liberty, skyscrapers – all in place, just like the brochure photographs. But for me, arrival was particularly poignant. My paternal grandfather, a would-be immigrant from a small Austrian farm, had got this far in the last century. No one came forward to collect him from Ellis Island, so he was shipped back to Liverpool and walked to London, to relatives, penniless and without a word of English.

But here we were, waving our British passports and immigrants' visas, being welcomed to the Brave New World with hoots, whistles, flags and bunting. I hoped Grandad was watching.

On 2 May 1953, there was the first of a series of three fatal accidents involving Comets on BOAC flights within twelve months. Later that month, Edmund Hillary and Tensing, a Sherpa, reached the summit of Mount Everest.

THAT SUMMER OF LOVE, 1957

Sheelagh was sixteen. She wore pumps and a ponytail, which she shook to this new music, rock'n'roll. Philip Norman was fourteen, and more conservative. One record by Buddy Holly changed everything.

The September of 1957 was a hot and noisy one in the Isle of Wight's Victorian seaside resorts. I spent it mainly pushing a slop trolley around my father's self-service cafeteria at the end of Ryde Pier, the second-longest pier in Britain. At that time, the only rhythms in my head came from the records we played as background music – Mantovani and his Orchestra; the aged Charlie Kunz's piano medleys of vaudeville songs like 'Shine on Harvest Moon'. I can still hear them in their sequence, tinkly and sentimental, almost lost against the clash of cutlery, the clatter of trays, the distant loudspeaker-boom of my father's voice inviting holidaymakers to forsake the sunshine for the shadows and doubtful pleasures of his establishment:

'Try today's two-shilling special hot lunch or salad in the self-service cafeteria on the ground floor. The entrance is on the tramway station. Make certain of your meal in comfort before you leave the pier . . .'

I was fourteen years old, and a more than usually abject specimen of late 50s British adolescence. Picture a youth with water-slicked hair and bowed shoulders, wearing a grubby white coat, black Rayon 'drainpipe' trousers, slightly mildewed, black lace-up shoes. Imagine the profoundest possible ignorance about everything going on in the outside world, combined with utter lack of animation, expectation or hope. We none of us know how unhappy we are until we have something to compare it with. For me, in those days, misery was seamless and horizonless; I thought that was how it felt to be alive.

You might think it a curious condition for a seaside showman's son, raised among penny-arcades, roller-skating rinks, sun-deck cafés and grand carnival dances. But my father was a seaside showman somewhat out of the ordinary. A former squadron leader in the Royal Air Force, addicted to gentlemanly pursuits like shooting and fly-fishing, he had come to the Isle of Wight seeking the quick fortune that allured so many ex-servicemen after the Second World War. As that quick fortune stubbornly eluded him, summer after summer, so did his hatred of his business, and of his customers, proportionately increase.

To my father, all pleasure, style and grace had ended with the 1930s. His was not the present, proletarian world of beer and candyfloss, but a vanished elegiac one of Oxford bags, 'Bullnose' Morris cars and schoolboy high jinks in the officers' mess. His favourite tense was the past historic: how things 'used to' be. From the age of nine or so, and especially since my parents' bitter and messy divorce, the same thought had visited me constantly. Everything worthwhile was over, and I'd missed it all. From here on, there was nothing to look forward to but ever-deepening anticlimax. The passage of time itself seemed to be getting slower, and some day soon must wind down to a complete stop.

That summer of 1957, I fell in love for the very first time. It seemed wholly typical of me that first love, far from being the elevating thing I had imagined, should bring still more extravagant plunges into despondency.

Her name was Sheila, spelt in the Irish way, 'Sheelagh'. She worked in the cafeteria's wash-up, where at intervals I unloaded my slop trolley's cargo of dirty plates and cutlery. She was a tiny girl with large brown eyes that protruded slightly, and lustrous mousy hair worn in a newly modish ponytail. There was something else, too, which I had not noticed until it was emphatically pointed out by my barmen and waiter colleagues. Tiny Sheelagh had the substantial, low-slung bust of a mature woman many times her height and weight. It was as if her wrap-around overall concealed a third arm, supported in a sling or pinned in a straitjacket.

Sheelagh was sixteen, an awesome two years senior. For all her childlike appearance, she seemed intimidatingly grown-up, with a knowledge of the world that painfully exposed my foggy, introverted ignorance. She had seen all the latest Hollywood films, like *The King and I*, starring Yul Brynner and Deborah Kerr, and was an attentive reader of glamour and gossip papers like *Reveille* and *Weekend Mail*. Her conversation was studded with topical film-star names that until then I'd barely registered – Tab Hunter, Russ Tamblyn, Sal Mineo, John Saxon and James Dean, whose death in a car crash the previous year had made him superlatively famous and fascinating.

When discussing any of these, Sheelagh's rather prim exterior would dissolve. The prominent brown eyes would bulge even further; a hand would be laid on the impressive bust to still the fluttering heart beneath; the pursed little mouth would utter a lovelorn sigh of 'Tab!' (or 'Russ!' or 'John!' or 'Sal!'). She talked endlessly, not only about the films they had made but about their cars, their clothes, their favourite foods, their possible true-life involvement with the leading ladies they kissed on-screen. On the latter subject, her tone became calmly proprietorial, as if it could be only a matter of time before Tab (or Sal or Russ or John) tired of glossy Hollywood starlets and realised that his true happiness lay with her.

For a fourteen-year-old swain, never before exposed to feminine wiles, those demonstrations of Sheelagh's were devastating. She liked John Saxon better than me. She liked Sal Mineo better than me. She even liked James Dean, someone dead, better than me. While she to me was a miracle of delicacy and mystery, I to her was the merest second-best substitute and stopgap. It turned out that she had meticulously planned her whole future, marriage, child-birth and domestic life in a sunlit, paradisiacal clime that clearly was nowhere near the Isle of Wight, with an imaginary partner bearing no resemblance to me. She talked about it all the time in words formalised into an incantation: 'I want a long white house and a long white car. And when I have a little boy, I'm going to name him Ashley.'

The greatest cultural gulf between us, and source of insecurity for me, was Rock 'n' Roll music. Sheelagh, of course, bore no resemblance to the wild 'Teddy girls', whom cinema newsreels occasionally showed whirling and cavort-ing to the horrendous new sounds. Even so, the merest mention of Elvis Presley or 'Britain's First Rock'n'Roller' Tommy Steele sent her into a miniaturised version of the same madness. She would stop dead in her tracks, bow her ponytailed head, cross her arms over her bust, stamp her little feet in their flat white pumps, and utter low, rhythmic moans of 'Oo! Oo! Oo! Oo! Oo!' while I stood helplessly by, riven with disgust at my failure to be comparably attractive or exciting.

I myself knew nothing about rock'n'roll, and wanted to know nothing. It was an obsession of the working-class masses that streamed down the pier to Ryde's beaches and pubs each summer day. It had nothing to do with boys like me who attended private schools, played rugby rather than football and wore blazers displaying mottoes in Latin. I accepted the adult view of it as just another ludicrous but passing American fad. Soon, even its most demented enthusiasts would realise the whole thing was a cynical confidence trick; that rock'n'roll performers like Elvis Presley couldn't really sing and only pretended to play the guitars that had become their essential props.

I waited impatiently for this revelation to dawn on Sheelagh. But, instead, more and more rock'n'rollers kept coming along to turn her head, both American originals and our hurried domestic imitations – Pat Boone, Paul Anka, Charlie Gracie, Russ Hamilton, Michael Holliday, the Most Brothers: 'England's answer to the Everly Brothers.'

'There are some new ones,' she announced one overcast September morning as we walked to work down the half-mile of pier planks, accompanied by her best friend, Diane White.

My first love spoke with a slightly softened 'r' that I was already having to struggle quite hard not to mimic to myself: 'They're called the Cwickets. They've got a gweat wecord out called "That'll Be The Day".'

Even to so unsporty an English boy as I was in 1957, the word 'cricket' was redolent of Test matches at Lord's and Headingley far more than the nocturnal buzzing of tropical climates. I had no idea who these Crickets might be or what they did. Their plurality made my heart sink; not one but several new rivals for Sheelagh's attention.

In that subtle way she had developed of fanning my possessive agony, she began to run through the record's lyrics with her friend Diane.

'"When Cupid shot his . . . something. He shot it at your heart." What wymes with heart?'

'Dart?'

'That's it. "When Cupid shot his dart . . . He shot it at your heart." What wymes with heart?'

'Fart?' suggested Diane, sending them both off into peals of laughter.

'No, "part". "When Cupid shot his dart . . . He shot it at your heart."' I realised that the words were being used to cut further ground from under my feet ' . . . And if we ever part and I leave you.'

I knew without even hearing them that I hated this record called 'That'll Be The Day' and these 'new ones', the Crickets. When I went to Sheelagh's house that following Sunday afternoon, I was dismayed to learn that she'd bought a copy and was intent on playing it for me. This duly happened in a tiny council house kitchenette, looking out on to open fields. I remember that as I prepared to listen, my chief sensation – stronger even than puppy love – was the familiar one of gnawing guilt. How could I be dallying selfishly here with a girl when I should be supporting my father's heroic efforts to keep bankruptcy at bay on the pier head?

Sheelagh slipped the newfangled, small unbreakable disc on to the turntable of her Dansette portable record-player, then she and her friend Diane joined hands and started to jive. This was a practice still considered almost indecent, and I was mortified to see how good Sheelagh was at it. She took the girl's much more complicated part, twirling at the end of Diane's outstretched arm, rotating and then expertly catching Diane's hand again, her ponytail swinging to and fro, white pumps scuffing loudly on the coconut mat. From time to time, she glanced across at me in a vaguely challenging way and murmured the refrain that was so apt a comment on my quest for her undivided heart: 'That'll be the day. Oo-oo! That'll be the day . . .'

Despite my pose of sulky indifference, there were things about the song I could not help noticing. The sound of the electric guitar – a concept still as exotic as thermonuclear fission – was more piercingly metallic than I'd ever heard before. In particular, that twanging, down-spiralling introduction, the utter distillation of rock'n'roll mayhem, fascinated me in ways I could not understand. The voice, by contrast, was low and reined back, eschewing all its later tricks of phrasing and inflection, barely separable from the blurry chorus of 'Oohs' and 'Aahs'. It struck me even then as perhaps not so very hard to imitate. And the name on the record label, Coral, struck an obscure chord of glamour and elegance.

Lead singers in rock'n'roll groups used not to be identified by name unless it was part of the billing, as with Frankie Lymon and the Teenagers. There was thus a mild novelty in hearing radio disc jockeys give the Crickets' vocalist separate mention as 'Buddy Holly'. Though nowhere near as bizarre a name as Elvis Presley, it still seemed curious, with that ungainly double 'y': the 'Buddy' as American as dungarees and drugstores, the 'Holly' so English, red-berried and prickly. No further details were forthcoming, however, not even when 'That'll Be The Day' went to number one in the Top 20. I didn't know – and the voice gave no clue – whether Buddy Holly was white like Presley and Bill Haley, or black like Fats Domino and Little Richard.

My first sight of him, like that first sound of him, I also owe to Sheelagh. Arriving at her house a few Sundays later, I found her and Diane poring over the sleeve of a long-playing record called *The Chirping Crickets*.

Against an unnaturally blue sky stood four figures in pale grey suits, white shirts and red ties, supporting between them the bodies of two brownish electric guitars. I guessed, correctly, that Buddy Holly must be second one from the right – the tallest one with the longest neck and the widest and toothiest grin, who wore glasses with the same pattern of not very smart half-frames as my own.

To make up for the glasses, his suit was by far the smartest of the four, the line of his shoulder the most natural, the set of his white shirt and thin red tie the most elegant. His coat had two pocket-flaps, one above the other, a detail normally associated with classic English hacking jackets. I realised that a rock'n'roller need not necessarily be a wild Technicolor freak, but could be clean-cut, smart, understated, even tidy. Though I had never met him, and never would, Buddy Holly told me something in that moment. He told me I hadn't missed everything as I'd always thought; that the 50s were not becalmed in time and winding slowly down to a stop. There was a future ahead – one which I had as much claim on as anyone else, and which promised to be every bit as exciting as my father had found the officers' mess at Upper Heyford. I knew I wouldn't be happy until I wore a suit like that, and I possessed a guitar, flat and two-horned like that, and could play the heavenly back-spiralling metallic intro to 'That'll Be The Day'. It was the moment I came alive. And I owe it to Sheelagh.

The summer of 1957 was the first in which none of Britain's railways had Third Class carriages.

STRANGERS ON A TRAIN, 1959

After being demobbed from national service, Craig Orr decided to make his own way home from Cyprus. The journey was an unforgettable adventure.

Days to do? Very few. The national serviceman's mantra. My mates were decorating their kitbags and working on the tans they would show off back home. But no troop ship for me. I had been making plans for months to take a local release, which meant that I would effectively be demobbed from the Army in Cyprus, where I had been stationed since Christmas 1957, and make my own way home.

Not that the Army made things easy. Nothing that deviated from the norm was ever easy in the Army. I think I was the first serviceman to request this route out since the end of the Cyprus emergency (1955–59) some months before, and at first no one took me seriously. But regulations are everything in the services, and I had discovered that local release was an option covered by regulations. So it was just a matter of persevering. The first requirement was a passport from the Governor of Cyprus and visas for Turkey and Greece. I would then pick up further visas for Yugoslavia and Bulgaria in Istanbul.

According to the note in my passport I had £45 to get me home. (In those far-off days any money you were taking out of the country was recorded in your passport.) So I decided on the short, cheap flight from Nicosia to Adana in southern Turkey. At the time, Nicosia was the great air hub of the eastern Mediterranean; after the Turkish invasion of 1974 and the subsequent division of the island, its airport was closed. These days, travellers aiming for Turkey must fly from Ercan in the north, while the shabby resort of Larnaca has taken over as principal airport for the official Republic of Cyprus in the south of the island.

My most vivid recollection of the flight aboard, I think, a Cyprus Airways DC-3 is that the human passengers were almost outnumbered by the livestock, mainly poultry. Chickens were also in evidence on the train that I picked up at Adana and which had probably started some days before in Baghdad or Basra. I can't swear that people were cooking on the train, but who knows? If there was a dining car I never found it. But at every stop – and there were many – kebabs, water and bread were available on the platform. Agatha Christie's Orient Express it was not.

Conversation was limited. I could get by in French and German, but my Turkish and Greek were limited to 'yes, please' and 'thank you'. The passengers in my compartment appeared to be all Turks, save one elderly man, who after several hours said something to me in what I took to be Arabic. One picked up snippets of Arabic in the forces, but they were not usually the sort of words suitable for polite conversation. So I tried French and German. No joy. More hours passed, and then my companion said something that sounded vaguely familiar.

I looked at him questioningly, and he repeated it. It was Latin. What these first words were I cannot now recall, but we did manage a conversation of sorts in the language of the Caesars, albeit with extended silences, until I left the train at Konya about halfway to Istanbul.

In the interests of economy I had intended to hitchhike home, which is why I had a ticket only as far as Konya. However, lifts in rural Turkey are not as easy to come by as on the A3 from London to Portsmouth. Nevertheless, I found a truck stop and two friendly drivers whose French was as mediocre as mine, and we trundled on to Istanbul.

21

I had scarcely said goodbye and thanks to my benefactors, and was drinking my first coffee in Istanbul, when I was approached by a young man who offered in halting English to buy me another coffee. His name was Ozben and he said he was a medical student. Could I help him with his English?

He turned out to be my guide for a week in Istanbul. He organised a student pass, accommodation and food. He took me to meet his family and showed me the sights. He even said that he could fix me a job teaching English if I wanted to stay on in Turkey. I was tempted, but it was nearly two years since I had left the UK and I was keen to get home. Ozben helped me to get transit visas for Bulgaria and Yugoslavia – no stopping in Eastern Europe in those days – and saw me off on the train heading for Sofia and Belgrade. Change there for Munich.

My only recollection of the capital of Bavaria was the huge new railway station, where I and other vagrants slept when we could avoid the attentions of the *Polizei* who wanted to move us on. A lady schoolteacher gave me a lift to Stuttgart, and from there I managed further lifts to Paris. It was my first visit to the French capital, but its delights were beyond my means, which by now were running rather low.

I worked out that if I didn't eat too much and got a lift to Dieppe I would just have enough cash to get the ferry to Newhaven and train or bus to Manchester. Customs gave me a serious going-over. I guess the Cyprus passport and several weeks of grime didn't help, but that wasn't the worst of the homecoming. The summer of 1959 had been the hottest in the UK for years. I arrived home to find that everyone had a tan as good as, or better than, mine. But crossing Europe a decade before the first hippies was well worth the effort.

In August 1959, Alec Issigonis unveiled the Mini. It was advertised as possessing an East/West engine.

FREE AT LAST TO KISS CHILDHOOD GOODBYE, 1959

In 1959 Anna Pavord left school, burned her beret and headed off to Norway for three months. When she returned, blonde and confident but slightly weepy, her parents did not recognise her.

The summer I left school, I looked much the same as when I started there, seven years previously. I still wore white ankle socks, Clark's sandals, a hideous tie of navy-and-gold stripes and an even more hideous beret with a gold badge on the front. Girls have ways with berets now and the art of customising a school uniform comes easily to an eighteen-year-old. Then, the year before the confident 60s began, there didn't seem to be ways with anything.

I left school with relief, had a ceremonial burning of the beret in our garden and almost immediately left for Norway, where a family friend had arranged an exchange with a Norwegian girl, Anne-Grethe Holm.

There had never been such freedom in my life as was represented by this three-month break before university in the autumn. The young now sensibly award themselves years off as though this were written into the educational curriculum: a year off between school and university; another between university and a job. I wish we had thought of that.

For me, Norway represented what India and Thailand became for subsequent waves of school-leavers. Not that it was on anybody's must-visit itinerary, but it symbolised escape from the known. I had never slept at sea before, as I did on the crossing from Newcastle to Bergen. I had never been in a place where I could not understand a word of what was being said to me. In fact, I had been abroad only once before and that was to France.

The summer of 1959 was remarkable for its heat. There have been heat waves since, but that one was the first that made any impression. The heat somehow was an integral part of the transmutation of that summer.

In Norway, I shed the ankle socks and padded about barefoot like the rest of the tribe of young people whose families summered on the fiord. Hardly front-page news, I know, but it was the beginning of a whole process of reinventing myself: the way I looked, the way people thought of me. Of course, there wasn't any grand plan. It wasn't even a conscious process, but cut off from everything I knew (a phone call home would have been an unthinkable extravagance), I became vividly aware that there were new and different ways of doing things.

The Holm family's wooden summer house was built by the side of a fiord, just outside Sandefjord. Their winter home was in the town, where Anne-Grethe's father disappeared to work every day. Below the summer house were rocks and a jetty; behind were woods of pine and birch. Perhaps half-a-dozen times that summer we went by car on an expedition; the rest of the time we spent on or in the water.

Having grown up deeply under the influence of *Swallows and Amazons*, I could swim, row and handle a sailing boat reasonably well. The new and wildly liberating angle to this in Norway was that it all happened without a grown-up in sight. No one shouted instructions about the best way to come alongside the jetty. No one told you what time you had to be in at night.

There must have been about twenty of us, all about the same age, knocking around in that summer's gang: nineteen

Norwegians and me. The fathers went off to Sandefjord each day; the mothers did I never discovered what; and we picnicked, sailed, fished, swam, made barbecues (my first), and every night partied at a different person's house – rowing or sailing ourselves home by the light of the moon at two or three o'clock in the morning. Elvis Presley provided the only common ground.

When you are crashing about as we were, it does not matter that you cannot converse deeply and meaningfully with your peers. You still communicate. You still pick up the undertow of what is going on in the group. I learned enough Norwegian to survive. The gang had enough English between them to fill in the gaps.

Some days we rowed with a picnic lunch to Longholm, a biggish island in the fiord, and swam and sunbathed until it got dark. Some evenings we would sit on the jetty with mussels tied to long pieces of string, fishing for crabs. The trick was to flip the line on to the jetty before the crab let go of the mussel. Then we tossed the crabs into a cauldron on the bonfire and ate them for supper.

We raced dinghies across the fiord, playing a slightly nerve-racking game of who dared be last to avoid the vertical rock face that fell down there into the water. We went to Seilholm for the regatta and sailed much bigger boats on a course that took us out of the fiord into the open sea.

We swam with Coca-Cola bottles on our heads (no one drank alcohol) out to an uninhabited scrap of island, sand and heather, where one of the boys – Petter? Roar? Turen? – taught me to rumba while the others beat out the rhythm with stones on the rocks. For heaven's sake! The rumba! On an uninhabited island! With a gang of people straight out of Ingmar Bergman's *Summer with Monika*! How liberated could you get in 1959?

I learned a lot from that gang. Mostly how to operate in one. It was the first holiday I had ever spent with a large, mixed group of people my own age. All holidays except the one in France had been with my parents. And in Norway I shed a lot of the muddling baggage that a single-sex education can leave you with: boys as Martians, to whom you speak and behave in a different way from your own sex. There were no couples in this group. All dressed in much the same way. I got my first pair of unisex jeans in Norway. Until then, like most girls in England, I had worn trousers that zipped up at the side. My front-buttoning pair were a sensation when I returned home.

I have learned since that I am only really happy on holiday in places where there are mountains. I didn't know that then, but they were there anyway. Even in Oslo, where I went at the end of the summer to stay with Anne-Grethe's cousin, Ellen, you could cycle easily from the centre of the capital out into the forest and mountains. It seemed eminently sensible that freedom and solitude (though I wasn't much into solitude at that time) should be within easy reach of all the people in the city.

We went to gaze at Edvard Munch's paintings, troubling even then, though I couldn't have said why. We went to admire the Viking ships. We walked frequently in the Frognerpark among Gustav Vigeland's monumental carvings. I heard the music of *West Side Story* for the first time in an Oslo flat. Finally I left for England by way of the Fred Olsen Line. Some of the gang came to Oslo to see me off, with bunches of carnations and roses that filled the hand-basin of my cabin.

On the way out, I had spent much of the journey in my cabin, not knowing where I was supposed to go to find food, scared that someone might try to strike up a conversation. I scarcely saw my cabin on the way back. Within an hour I had fallen for a lanky, fair- haired, green-eyed Norwegian boy called Tore. We played cards, liar dice, drank Tom Collins (my first gin), and stayed up all night dancing to a gramophone in the saloon. The barman thought I was Norwegian, too. We never told him the truth. There's neither time nor the opportunity to fall in love on an aeroplane, but boats are good for romance.

Part of the romance was to bring the thing to an end at Newcastle. Affairs rarely have such neat conclusions. I hated seeing England again: drab Newcastle, filthy train, grey weather. I cried all the way to Birmingham, where my parents had arranged to meet me. I stood on the platform with my huge suitcase, watching my father and mother working their way towards me. I smiled, stepped forward – and they walked straight past me.

'But your hair!' said my mother later, trying to explain why she had failed to recognise her only daughter. 'It's gone so fair!' That was true. After a lifetime of mousy brownness, my hair was bleached clear blonde by a summer of sea and sun. 'And you are so brown!'

That was true, too; but the real change, the reason they did not know me on the platform of Birmingham New Street, was much more complex. In Norway I had shut the lid on childhood and started the business of being grown-up.

Britain's first duty-free shops opened on 17 November 1959, at Glasgow's two airports, Prestwick and Renfrew.

TIZER, GOLD LEAF AND NUCLEAR FALLOUT, 1962

Simon Calder recalls his first overseas trip – more of an evacuation than a holiday.

No one remembers how much it cost. British Airways has no record of the fare from Gatwick to Guernsey over forty years ago. At the time, my parents honestly didn't care about the expense: two-and-four-halves to the Channel Islands was soon buried in the family overdraft, and anyway it was a small price to pay for life insurance.

The Tornadoes were number one in the charts with 'Telstar', a curiously timely instrumental jangle celebrating the latest US satellite. High above the Caribbean, American spy aircraft were photographing missile silos in Cuba, and nuclear warheads on Soviet ships were steaming towards the island. In capital cities thousands of miles away, tension was rising between Nikita Krushchev, Fidel Castro and Jack Kennedy. Anxiety was growing in our house too, since we lived only a couple of miles from the runway at Gatwick. Mum, Dad, Penny, Sarah, Jo and I would be prime targets in a nuclear conflict. We knew American planes were not strangers to Gatwick, because we'd waved President Kennedy off from there aboard Air Force One after his visit to Britain a year earlier. So it was reasonable to assume that a Soviet missile was pointing at the airport – and our house. Evidence that has emerged since the collapse of the USSR suggests my parents were right to fear imminent destruction in 1962.

'We were quite convinced there was going to be a nuclear war,' my father recalls, 'and felt you lot had to be taken to safety.'

We children couldn't comprehend the notion that some-one might want to obliterate our peaceful universe, and what's more we didn't much care – we were going on an AEROPLANE. A BEA Vickers Viscount whisked us from Gatwick to Guernsey in what seemed like five minutes; having repeated the journey paying the adult fare, I have to report that the same journey now takes an hour, aboard more modern aircraft. Yet the overall journey time is much longer, because of the need to go through security, and wait our turn in the queue of planes waiting to take off from what is now the world's busiest single-runway airport.

My parents did their best to explain why we had suddenly changed from an impecunious, non-car-driving, non-TV-owning household into a jet-setting family. I thought I understood their rationale, but there was one nagging concern about their gentle explanation of impending doom: if we were trying to get away from an airport because it was a potential target, why on earth had we *flown* somewhere – Guernsey airport seemed just as grand as Gatwick. The complexities of strategic warfare were beyond a six-year-old.

When I grew old enough to comprehend the horror of what we were trying to escape, I assumed we'd gone to Guernsey just because it was the closest and cheapest destination away from the mainland. In fact, my parents had given the matter a great deal of thought. In the course of his work as a science writer, my father had learned of a water-desalting plant in Guernsey – potentially useful in the aftermath of a nuclear attack. 'Also an island seemed a good place to avoid the marauding hordes after the war,' he adds. However unusual the reasons for our choice of holiday destination, we had a wonderful time and encountered no marauding hordes. The landscapes were glorious sweeps of bold colour, scenery lifted from a storybook. The deep greens of the fields, the gold of the sand and the sunsets, and the blues of the sky and the sea defied any ordinary spectrum. Better still, ice cream and Tizer were in limitless supply. I also noted my parents' glee on discovering that Player's Gold Leaf were duty-free.

For a week the world held its breath on the brink of World War III, while we ate, drank and went our merry childish way. 'There was a bus stop right outside the hotel,' my mother remembers, 'and we never had to wait more than five minutes for a bus to anywhere on the island.' The nuclear threat diminished as we shuttled and snacked across Guernsey. Was it really like that? In the intervening years I have visited Cuba many times, but have returned to Guernsey only once. Gratifyingly, the island seems trapped in an early 1960s time warp.

The capital is St Peter Port, a jolly and overgrown fishing village protected by Castle Cornet, perched on a rock out to sea. Handsome granite houses stumble down Tower Hill to the town centre. Here, the Market Halls comprise a grand Victorian melange of wrought iron and graceful glass. The market stalls overflow almost into the pews of the Town Church, which sprawls in an ungainly but quaint fashion from its medieval heart. Even aged six, I sensed there was something odd about Guernsey. The street names are pure Franglais: Couture Water Lanes and Allez Street. Guernsey lies within the protective embrace of Cherbourg and the Cotentin peninsula, much closer to the French shore (30 miles) than the English coast (70 miles). The Channel Islands were part of William the Conqueror's feudal fiefdom when he invaded England. Territory has changed hands between France and England regularly in the past millennium, and somehow when the music stopped we were left with les Îles Normandes.

Guernsey's present bus service bears little relation to the high-frequency network my mother recalls, so I rented a bicycle (without stabilisers). The ride around the island was a comforting confirmation of half-remembered images, soft hills painted with the same broad sweeps of colour. In 1962, of course, the island was much bigger. But as journeys back in time go, it was a treat. Guernsey has no beaches to match those in Cuba, but the coastline is lovely: jagged fingers of rock jab out at the Channel, and the horizon is decorated by the neighbouring islands of Herm and Sark.

Havana boasts a Museum of the Revolution, complete with a 'Cretin's Corner' featuring George Bush. In Guernsey, the German Occupation Museum commemorates the last world war. The Channel Islands fell into Nazi hands, and the museum occupies bunkers left by the Germans; these could have been useful had the Cuban missile crisis become a full-scale war. From here a path leads to the tiny bay of Petit Bot, along a ravine draped in dense foliage. The intensity of colour and smell is almost tropical, like the forest on the fringes of Cuba's Bay of Pigs.

The food in Guernsey is megatons better than in Cuba, too. The Café de l'Escalier, at the top of one of St Peter Port's many staircases, serves excellent French cuisine, though the accordion music is a little oppressive. You need not look far for nightlife in Guernsey. Duty-free lager louts maraud around the town centre, and on Friday night every pub seems to be staging a Young Drinkers' Convention. The music on the jukebox is considerably older than the clientele, and I think I might have caught a snatch of 'Telstar'. Four decades on, Fidel Castro has survived Jack Kennedy, Che Guevara and the Soviet Union. The threat of nuclear annihilation seems to have subsided. My parents still live a couple of miles from the runway at Gatwick airport. And Guernsey hasn't changed a bit.

The first successful hijack of a US domestic flight to
Havana, Cuba took place four days before the end of 1961.
By the summer of '62, the practice had become
commonplace, and led to the introduction of security
screening of airline passengers.

FRESH TO THE UNIVERSITY OF LIFE, 1963

Tim Salmon looks back on his bohemian days on Crete in 1963.

Summer 1963. Did it change my life? It certainly set me on a path I've been following ever since.

I was 21. I'd just left Oxford, where I had successfully avoided ever entering the Union, having tea or even boarding a punt. I had secured a place to train as a Classics teacher, mainly to deflect my father's attempts to get me to embark on a sensible career. But I wrote a polite letter saying I wouldn't be coming, withdrew my forty quid savings from the post office and set off for Greece. Modern Greece, a friend used to say with gentle irony, for it is true that no one but classicists went to Greece in those days.

I had a suitcase, a guitar, a typewriter, a head full of notions about writing and a vague plan to get my French girlfriend to join me. It was a move I had been planning since 1960 when several months hitchhiking in Italy and Greece had given me a taste for the university of life, reinforced by heavy doses of Lawrence Durrell, Henry Miller and Hemingway.

I went by train. If there were any flights in those days, I never heard of anyone taking them. As we turned south into the Balkans it got hotter and progress slower. Through Yugoslavia the train stopped and started inexplicably. Hens scavenged on the line. In Salonica it stopped altogether. There was a strike and I had to continue to Athens by bus.

I went to the Hotel Byron in Odos Aiolou, with a view straight up to the Erychtheium, and booked a room on the roof for 17 drachmas. It was baking hot. Most of the guests were very indolent women who were not particularly youthful and never seemed to get dressed. The corridors were full of the odours of defective plumbing.

In the morning I went down to Odos Athinas, to one of those old-fashioned milk shops (extinct now) with marble-topped tables and straw-bottomed chairs, where I drank a bottle of milk and spooned a sickly sweet paste of honey and white, greasy butter on to chunks of fresh bread. The streets were crowded with men in sombre-coloured clothes. The boys, skulls shaven against lice, wore baggy shorts and hand-me-downs, the girls looked prim in dark pinafores and white socks.

I had the address of two Englishmen living on the edge of Plaka. I looked them up. They were out. 'In a café on the square,' someone told me. I found them playing chess: Gerry and Thomas. Gerry lives scarcely a mile from me now. Thomas, poor lad, the *Independent*'s man in Athens, died in 1993 after thirty years of passionate involvement with Greece.

I moved in with them, sleeping in the wash house on the roof. They were giving English lessons to make ends meet. But they could not afford underpants and their timetables were complicated by the need to meet between lessons to exchange the jacket they shared before appearing at some bourgeois apartment in Kolonaki.

At night we went into Plaka and drank and talked books. There was no tourist razzmatazz then; it was just a crumbling working-class district. There was a girl too, dark-haired Miranda, whom I picked up with drunken boldness one evening as she dined with her mother. She drank, too, and we climbed over the Acropolis railings to canoodle under the stars.

My money ran out and I had to look for a job. With the luck of youth I found one in a couple of days: teaching in a language school in Hania, Crete. We had a party on the eve of my departure. I left with a hangover and an aching heart. Miranda accompanied me to the airport, very pale and silent.

The first morning was frightening. It was a Sunday, I think, and in the quiet the blinding light and scarce-moving shadows seemed only to deepen my sense of solitude. But fear quickly gave way to pleasure. You are not allowed to be alone in Greece and very soon I was taken in hand by some young men of my own age. Who was I? What was I doing? Foreigners were almost unknown in Greece then, except as classicists and soldiers in foreign armies. And Hania was beautiful: quiet and provincial but full of vestiges of former elegance and grandeur (Venetian bastions and rusticated stonework, marble Turkish fountains, *hammams* and minarets) mouldering gently under the sun without affectation or pomposity, just part of the fabric of life.

I rented a room in an old house belonging to the aunt of one of my new friends. Bare boards, iron bedstead, a tin bowl to wash in, and heavy, wooden shutters stripped of paint by sun and sea air. I moved after a few days, and lost a friend: I had offended his *filotimo* – that touchy sense of *amour-propre* that made Cretans so quick to feud.

I had met John Craxton one night in a barrel-lined taverna. He was talking Greek and it was only when I heard him say Charlie Mingus – not a name you expected to hear on the lips of Haniotes – that I guessed he might be English. He'd been there for years already, a real live painter, with canvases in the Tate; he was a friend of Paddy Leigh Fermor, legendary hero of the Cretan Resistance, for whose books he still designs the jackets. He found me a room in a far finer house close to the harbour. And through him I met other members of the small foreign community: mostly aspiring writers and painters. One of them, an American, had just published his first novel: my first real writer.

Another was murdered not long after, in gruesome circumstances. They were all older than me and many were gay, not that the word meant that then. They lived what, I suppose, was a pretty bohemian existence by the standards of the day. For me it was the big time.

I owe much to John. He was fascinated by all things Cretan: history, music, customs, architecture, artefacts, landscape. And he passed that on to me. Through him I went to the mountains, to Sfakia, cradle of rebels and warriors against the Turks. Through him I was invited to a big mountain wedding where we fetched the bride from her home, firing rifles into the air, and drank and danced all day and night to the frenetic twanging of the Cretan lyre, and the guests sang traditional *mantinadhes* back and forth antiphonally between bride's guests and groom's guests. Through him, too, I acquired four ancient Cretan chairs, one of which I am sitting on now, sprouting grass in the courtyard of a mountain café. At night we sat in the harbour drinking ouzos at two drachmas a shot, and each one accompanied by plates of fish, sea urchins, olives and cheese, without any extra charge. At weekends the sailors came into town from the naval base at Souda and drank and danced on the backs of the chairs and lifted fully laid tables in their teeth, without spilling a drop of the wine.

Work played little part in my life. I taught just three or four hours in the evening. On my first day I was taken aside by the doorman.

'Young man,' he said, 'you be careful with the girls or you'll have their brothers to contend with.' And he drew his thumb graphically across his throat. They were demure and shyly flirtatious but quite inaccessible.

One evening I met a black American airman on leave from the US base at Heraklion and we became friends. We were both much taller than the average Cretan and little knots of girls would form, and giggle and look at us in the streets. He would take me to the red-light district where he seemed to be well known, though he never did anything while I was around and I was much too timid. We would call on one or two rather sexy young women he knew. One came to the top of the stairs to speak to us in nothing but her knickers. Not a sight I had been accustomed to in the English countryside or boarding schools. On Saturdays we went to the bouzouki joint and rock'n'rolled lecherously with girls of dubious reputation.

Summer stretched into autumn. I moved into a house overlooking the harbour. King Paul processed beneath my balcony in celebration of the fiftieth anniversary of Crete's union with Greece. I dreamed of writing a thriller about shooting him. Elections were held, which were won by George Papandreou, father of Greece's former PM, breaking the hold of the right for the first time since the civil war of 1946–49. I have a photograph of him in front of my house in the company of Constantine Mitsotakis, Greece's last PM, whose desertion from his party led eventually to the colonels' coup in 1967. Earlier in the year Grigoris Lambrakis, a left-wing MP and CND activist, had been murdered by right-wing thugs as he left a rally in Salonica, the subject of Costa-Gavras's film Z.

Dark-haired Miranda wrote to say she wanted to come and stay. So did my French girlfriend, and I plumped for her. Fred Perles arrived to join our community. He had lived with Henry Miller in Paris in the 1920s and had known all manner of exotic figures, like Anais Nin and Lawrence Durrell. He would read Miller's letters to us, in which, disappointingly, the grand old man spoke chiefly of his incontinence.

Michael Cacoyannis arrived to make *Zorba The Greek*, with Anthony Quinn and Irene Papas. Hania thought it had become the centre of the universe.

One day I was asked to stand in for Anthony Quinn. I thought my time had come, until I discovered that the man was indisposed and they needed someone roughly the same height so as to adjust the lighting. In pique, I declined the invitation.

These great ones used to dine in our neighbourhood taverna. One night I went in to find them seated, as usual, at a long table with Quinn at one end and, at the other, a little barefooted boy called Orestes, who sold peanuts. He sat, full of self-possession, with his feet on a bar of his chair, a plate of food in front of him, and his nose in a Greek newspaper, which he was perusing, very seriously, upside down.

My girlfriend arrived, much to the delight of Fred. He was half-French and had an eye for the girls; one of his outrageous sallies is quoted under 'Breasts' in *The Joy of Sex*. One day I met him in the hotel where we used to go for occasional baths, as none of us had hot water, let alone a bath, at home. I told him we were going to get married. He looked me in the eye. 'Tim,' he said, 'if you want a glass of milk, you don't buy a cow!' and continued up the stairs.

That summer stretched, in fact, into a year and, indeed, into a lifelong involvement with Greece. For although I left Crete in 1964 to train as a teacher of English and ended up first in Libya, then in London, I went back to Greece in the 70s and stayed for fourteen years, marrying a Greek in the process. My Oxford tutor, hearing of my doings from a friend, commented: 'That fellow, Salmon . . . rolling stone.' If it's true, I certainly seem to have gathered a lot of moss.

On President Kennedy's visit to Britain in the year he died, Air Force One chose to land at Gatwick Airport rather than Heathrow.

NORTHERN EXPOSURE, 1963

Does your mother know? The 60s are famous for sex, drugs and rock'n'roll. But for Barbara Butler, they heralded a journey to the Arctic Circle.

I was nineteen and setting off on my first solo trip abroad. Inger, my Swedish pen friend, had been to stay with me in Huddersfield and now, in return, she had invited me back to Sweden. My itinerary was to be a few days in Stockholm, a short trip to Malmberget above the Arctic Circle, and then back to Inger's home in Strangnas, west of Stockholm. One of the main things on my mind as I packed was what to wear – such an important thing for a teenager. Not trousers, as I'd have chosen now, but a neat, light-blue, linen suit with navy-blue court shoes and a bag – possibly even cotton gloves.

What an impact Scandinavia was about to make. It is still easy to recall because it made such vivid impressions on my senses. Not many of smells though – certainly not in the toilets, where there were dispensers of antibacterial wet-wipes for the loo seat (unheard of in the parts of Britain I'd frequented) – just of sunshine and vegetation and tastebud-tempting meatballs.

There were so many new tastes: compotes of berry fruits, smorgasbords stuffed with treats – fantastic pickles and rollmop herrings, novel breads and crispbreads – and breakfasts filled with strange new flavours – yoghurt (not so common in Britain then) served with cornflakes and, less temptingly, porridge made with rice.

As to sounds, I remember birdsong, bits of conversations – notably a hunky friend of Inger's telling me, 'You look beautiful when you smile' – and the train rushing along, carrying me to the far north. The train itself was light years ahead of those running in Britain at the time (and probably still is, even now, more than four decades later).

Mainly, though, I just remember that there was a wonderful lightness and airiness in the wide, open landscapes – the huge, colourful meadows of the south and the seemingly endless spread of tundra in the north – and in the buildings and design. Whether old or new, the decoration all seemed fresh and soft on the eye. Everything appeared to be pastel-coloured, from the paintwork on city walls to the furniture and tiles in the grand, old palaces we visited (I was especially impressed by the elegant Royal Palace at Drottningholm, which is close to Stockholm) and homes such as Inger's.

I was fascinated by the differences in decoration between this modern Swedish flat and houses I knew in Yorkshire. Everything in Sweden seemed to be so new, efficient and streamlined, and the flat was no exception. Simple yet ergonomically functional, it was upholstered in textiles of neat, abstract designs. The decoration was along very modern, rather minimalist, lines, with windows that were made private by blinds and loose, open-weave curtains that sensibly allowed as much light as possible to filter through – such a contrast to the lace curtains and heavy drapes in vogue in Yorkshire.

Somehow I managed to drag myself away from the swishness of Inger's flat, and we went to see the vast hulk of the *Vasa* in Stockholm. The massive – and magnificent – warship had sunk on its maiden voyage in 1628, before it even left the boundaries of the city's harbour but, two years before I visited, it had been sucked out of the mud to huge public enthusiasm. These days it sits regally – and fully restored – in a grand museum, but in 1963 it was still under conservation and had to be constantly sprayed with a fine jet of water to preserve its timbers.

It was the detail that had got me hooked, from the shimmering, interior walls of the Civic Hall, covered in gold leaf, to the white boulders that defined the Arctic Circle as we passed by to glimpse the unforgettable midnight sun. How hard to come down to earth, to put on that light-blue suit and head for home. One accessory I wouldn't be without in future was that smile.

In 1963, the RAC followed the lead of the AA: its patrolmen stopped saluting motorists who were members of the Club.

GOING WILD IN WALES, 1963

It may be livelier today, but Tenby retains the charm. Richard Evans remembers from a childhood visit.

The lads' mag *Maxim* once voted it the second-best place in the world for stag nights. It has golden sands and a vibrant nightlife. But this is not Miami or even Prague, but Tenby in Pembrokeshire. Portrayed in recent years in the tabloids as a town at war with marauding crowds of drunks, it all sounded a far cry from the rather genteel resort I remember from my childhood in the 60s.

A week in one of the Victorian hotels on The Esplanade overlooking Tenby's South Beach was something different. It was the first time I'd stayed in a hotel – let alone in one with two stars. Every morning we climbed down steep steps to the beach, swam in the sea, built sandcastles and played in rock pools and caves. We took a boat trip to see the monks on Caldey Island and brought back sweets in a jar. Afterwards a man in a white jacket served us supper on crisp linen tablecloths with heavy cutlery. Someone made the bed for us and folded up clothes we left on the floor. I can still remember the smell of the suntan oil and the sheets as I was dropping off to sleep, the call of the sea and the gulls and the sand I brought back from the beach with me.

I was pleased to find that trains still come down from Swansea – winding along the coast and then cutting discreetly through the Carmarthenshire countryside. These days they are powered by diesel, and are just one or two carriages long rather than the steam-hauled beauties of the Great Western Railway that used to bring in holidaymakers by the thousand. What's left of Tenby railway station is a couple of minutes' walk from the medieval town walls, into which have been poured the pastel-coloured Regency terraces, the shops, the pubs and the restaurants. On one side the narrow streets spill down towards the North Beach and the old harbour; on the other, they clamber down to the sweep of the South Beach. It's still safe and clean, with golden sand, first-class bathing and views across the bay – and Fecci's ice cream.

There are amusement arcades and shops selling beach paraphernalia, but it's not like the more vulgar resorts of the English south coast. In Tenby, the slot machines are tucked away behind modest shop fronts. Boats still take tourists to Caldey Island where the Cistercian monks sell visitors chocolate and perfume made from wild flowers. The Pembrokeshire Coastal Path winds east to Amroth, but to the west, past the testing golf course in the sand dunes, there's another hundred miles or so to St Bride's Bay with its remote rocky coves, seabirds and cliff-top walks.

There were no crisp tablecloths at lunch anymore, but there were lamb sausages and plenty of local fish; the cobbled lanes meander down to the harbour where the day's catch is still sold on the quayside. The sun shone for our return, but then they say this sheltered corner of Carmarthen Bay is lucky with the weather.

If you find yourself caught by one of the systems sweeping in from the Atlantic, all will not be lost however. Within walking distance there's the 15th-century merchants' house and Saint Mary's parish church – one of the largest in Wales. Henry Tudor hid in the vaults before fleeing to France and returning as king.

On Castle Hill, with its views over the beaches to the north and to Caldey in the south, the museum tells more tales of ships and lifeboats. The art gallery proudly shows off the paintings of Augustus John, the local boy who grew a beard and went a bit bohemian after a diving accident, going on to become one of the most important artists of his generation. His legacy lives on in scores of little art shops, potteries and galleries in the area. The scenery of the National Park is a landscape artist's dream.

Saturday nights in high season can get rowdy, but rarely threatening, and no more than in the 70s according to my sister-in-law, who tended to the wayward in her youth. She tells me, with a distant grin, that it was all going on in Cinderella's. My mother went back to that hotel on The Esplanade a few years ago and said it wasn't what it used to be. But I am glad to report that the resort of Tenby is still a little gem.

In 1963, Dr Richard Beeching was made Chairman of the British Railways Board. He ordered the closure of 5,000 miles of track and one in three stations.

THE HITCHHIKER'S GUIDE TO THE FALLACY, 1967

Seduced by his friends' tales of laughing peasants and lively girls, Neil Lyndon hit the road for the summer of love. The road hit back.

In the early summer of 1967, while my Cambridge friends were grooving in their beads and tie-dyes out of squats in Portobello Road and talking ganja and free love, I was working five-and-a-half days a week in a scrap-metal yard in Bristol and sighing out the last wearisome weeks of an engagement to be married to the love of my school years. We lived in her flat in Redland, impersonating marriage, watching black-and-white television in the evenings and playing *Sgt Pepper* on her Pye record player, trying to time our orgasms with the last chord at the end of the orchestral crescendo.

Our joint income must have been nearly £50 a week (maybe £600 or £700 today); but her work as a secretary made her bored, and my work wiped me out. The scrap yard was like the set of a Sam Shepard movie. Each working day at 8 a.m., risking tetanus with every handhold, I had to scale mountainous heaps of piping and panelling, planks of high-tensile steel and rusting car bodies, to reach the powered guillotine where I worked until 6 p.m. cutting metal into lengths and chunks. No gloves or overalls were provided, so my jeans and shirts became stiffly grimed with filthy oil and rust and the flesh of my hands blackheaded with metal splinters. The yard had no place to wash, so I travelled home on the bus looking like a miner up from the face. 'Mind your backs, ladies,' shouted the conductor one evening. 'Here comes the working man.'

One Saturday afternoon, I came home with fish and chips for lunch. My girlfriend was out. I put the food in the oven, spread some sheets of newspaper on the floor and dropped into a pit of sleep in my working clothes. When she came in, the food was cold in the oven, which I had forgotten to light, and the room was thick with the stink of sweat and old oil. She whined. I left. I was not going to spend any more of my first long vacation in a mockery of our parents' bitching cohabitations. I was off on the Grand European Hitch. Farewell marriage; hi-ho silver lining for the open road.

All the boys at Cambridge had done the hitch, to Venice, Athens, Kabul, Goa. I had listened covetously through the winter to their stories, ruefully contrasting the abundant hipness of their experiences with my own sorry sub-marital state. In India, they had fallen in with swamis; in Kabul with dealers in dope and carpets; in Florence they had met a young widow with a white Mercedes who let them drive to her flat in Munich where they made love day and night for weeks before she took them to Cannes to meet Alain Delon and Mick Jagger at parties. They had lived for months with no money, fed by laughing peasants in Italy and Greece who took them in. They had met a girl on the night ferry on the Adriatic who had done it with them under a tarpaulin on the deck. They had drawn sketches of St Sophia in Istanbul and had lain beneath the stars in Isfahan where Alexander walked. I had dragged myself round Tesco in Whiteladies Road for a basket full of Harpic, frozen chicken and Chianti.

Two boys from my college were driving their father's Mini to Athens. For a share of the petrol they agreed to take me as far as Rijeka, where I would meet Bob and Dick, my two best friends of that year, following which, according to our detailed imaginary itinerary, we would cast our seed broadly upon the Balkan states and hitchhike slowly and separately back through Europe, carried by the luck that our sensational good looks guaranteed us.

The boys in the Mini were careful chemists. They wore flannels and short-sleeved shirts and sandals. I wore my Levis, Cuban-heeled boots and a paisley-patterned pyjama top which, I had deluded myself, looked like the Liberty shirts that even the Small Faces were wearing that summer. (Everyone who saw me asked, 'Why are you wearing your pyjamas?') The chemists had a tent, sleeping bags, a Primus, a tin-opener and a box of beans. I had packed my old canvas cricket bag with a pullover, some pants and (following the advice of a vegan friend) a plastic bag containing three pounds of nuts, raisins and oat flakes.

This diet had blocked my pipes by the time we got to Lyons and was all eaten before Milan. 'Too bad,' said the boys, opening another tin of chipolatas.

They had written out a daily target of miles, to get to Athens in a hurry. They were doing Europe as a study in physical endurance and mechanical motion. I do not remember that we stopped to look at anything. While they drove, I sat in the back, smoking untipped Player's and reading *The New Left Manifesto* by Raymond Williams and Terry Eagleton, and a book about the theory of allegorical meanings, whose title and author I have forgotten. Little communication passed between the front and rear seats apart from demands for petrol money, conceded with ever-growing reluctance as the small wad in my jeans narrowed. In a northern Italian market town, I bought a dark-brown straw hat with a huge brim that I turned down in the shape of a Vietnamese peasant's paddy-field headwear. This drew eyes away from the pyjama jacket and was the envy of all.

Dick and Bob were waiting in Rijeka, tanned and merry with tales from the road: the polished routine, including lively girls and lovely food. Their luck must have run out when I joined them. Three Australian girls, heavy and plain and worried about their make-up, were on the ship. Hungry for sex, we made up to them when the boat left but our ardour waned when it hit an Adriatic storm and we were sick while the girls touched up their lipstick. We stopped for two days on the island of Hvar, then undeveloped, where I got sunstroke and Bob and Dick left me fainting in the street while they went to a restaurant for dinner. I could afford and stomach nothing more than melon.

On the walls of Dubrovnik, some ten-year-old girls mistook Dick's big mouth for Mick Jagger's and screamed. On the beach, I played ball for ten minutes with a girl so thin she made Twiggy look like Anita Ekberg. When she put the ball down, I propositioned her. She was astounded. 'You English boys are not human,' she said. That was the closest we came to sexual adventure.

My money ran out after three days in Dubrovnik. Kilburn High Road, not Isfahan, was calling. When I walked out of the town to find the road going north, I had one dinar in my pocket, the equivalent of seven old pence (£0.03). I saw a man watering his vegetables and asked for a drink. He roared at me to drop dead.

I settled on a place to hitch at the beginning of a long straight where I could watch the cars winding towards me round the mountain turns. I stood there for a day and a half. On the morning of the second day, I saw a white Mercedes 300 convertible approaching. As it turned into the straight, I saw that it was being driven by a blonde woman, alone in the car. Cautiously, as if pushing apart the veils of *déjà vu*, I held out my thumb. The car slowed. Then it accelerated past me. A drunk in a Fiat 500 stopped five hours later.

At 5.30 a.m. in Mostar, as I walked along the road on a broken heel, a man came out of some olive trees and punched me in the face. We staggered away from each other without speaking. At midnight in Sarajevo, while I was sleeping in a graveyard, a pack of wild dogs attacked me. I spent my last dinar on an ice cream near Zagreb and left Yugoslavia in an old van whose engine boiled over as it panted into the mountains.

Near Geneva, in the early evening, a man scented with drink and aftershave picked me up in a white Citroen DS21 and, seeing my weakness and fatigue, offered to take me home. Demurring, I fell asleep and awoke to find his hand on my thigh. I pushed it away. He hit my face with the back of his hand. I opened the door. He stopped the car and I fell out into a deluge like a high-pressure hose, which drenched my clothes and everything in my cricket bag in seconds.

At Versailles, I went to sleep on a park bench where a gendarme woke me with a kick in the groin at 4 a.m. North of Paris, a Morris Minor full of happy English kids stopped to take me to Calais where a perky stewardess on the ferry gave me a free meal, my first since Dubrovnik, in return for spending her money on my duty-free allowance. The Morris Minor dropped me in Kilburn High Road, fifty yards from a friend's front door. Within a week, I had got a job with a light-engineering factory. The engagement ring we had bought for ten quid came back in the post and I hocked it for five pounds. In October, when I got back to college, I told lies about young widows in white Mercedes convertibles.

Queen Elizabeth 2, the last transatlantic liner to be built in Britain, was launched on the Clyde on 20 September 1967. Her successor, *Queen Mary 2*, was built at St Nazaire in Brittany and entered service in 2004.

LOVE ON THE ROCK, 1968

Union Jacks, English pubs and chaps wearing blazers –
Gibraltar seems like a throwback to a different era. But, asks
Virginia Ironside, is reality finally catching up with the
disputed territory?

I was 24 years old when I last visited Gibraltar. We started
our journey at the air terminal in Cromwell Road, west
London, now the site of a giant Sainsbury's. We had flown
on a huge BEA aircraft. It wasn't Gibraltar we'd been after;
no, we were Morocco-bound, Nina, Peter and I, but in those
days it was cheaper to fly overnight to Gibraltar and then take
the ferry to Tangiers.

In 1968 British travellers were allowed to take no more
than £50 abroad – a sum that, though it went further in those
days than today, was still a pittance to take on holiday. (Peter
and Nina took the regulation amount; but when he got rolled
on his first night on the beach, Peter was delighted to find
that I had secretly smuggled an extra £30 in my suitcase.)

We had booked ourselves into a vile Gibraltarian hotel,
where we had to sleep three to a room, and, to pass the time
before the Tangiers ferry left, we walked around the dismal
British colony in the morning. Our memory was of fences
painted in red, white and blue, Union Jacks hanging from
every window; even gardens had been planted in England
colours – with white alyssum, red geraniums and blue
lobelia.

It was, as Nina remembers, the 'most frightful place, full
of elderly blokes in white shorts and naval shirts, cheery
bobbies, red pillar boxes, and all dominated by Main Street,

a mixture of Tottenham Court Road and Blackpool, which was lined with a mixture of electrical and camera shops, English pubs advertising fish and chips and mushy peas, models of Beefeaters and stuffed Gibraltar apes'. The nationalism depressed us then – but the Gibraltarians could hardly be blamed, because the following year Franco closed the borders and Gibraltar was isolated for seventeen years until the frontiers were reopened.

In those days, of course, we couldn't get out of there quick enough. Tangiers was amazing. Nina met her first husband, and got married to him a few weeks later, carried into the reception area on a huge golden plate; I found a taxi-driver boyfriend called Habbadi, and Peter had a series of young men who would melt into the morning the moment us girls appeared.

Treading the same ground more than thirty years later I found the situation almost completely reversed. Instead of staying at a beastly three-bedroom hostel, I put up at the Rock Hotel, a wonderful piece of 1930s architecture, all polished brass and palm trees, with a swimming pool and a man playing Gershwin on a piano in the restaurant. I was following in the footsteps of such illustrious – and poignantly dated – guests as Sir John Mills, Winston Churchill, Errol Flynn, Anna Neagle, Trevor Howard, the Prince of Wales and Moira Shearer.

Main Street has been pedestrianised and, except on the days when the tourist ships come in and about 5,000 football fans are disgorged on to the streets to buy gin at £5 a litre (no duty and no tax), goggle at Barbary apes and queue to go to the top of the Rock by cable car, the place has enormous 50s charm.

When I asked about the hot news of the moment (putting aside the hottest which is, of course, whether Gib remains British or not), which is whether women can serve on juries

– so far they are all-male – I was told: 'Of course we have equal rights here!' The genial bloke who was speaking wore a blazer bright with brass buttons, a huge silk spotted handkerchief bursting from the pocket. 'As long as the women know that the men are best! Ho! Ho! Ho!'

But because you know it's all going to change, that the Gibraltarians, with their weirdly old-fashioned views, are a dying race, that they are no longer a threat – as they appeared to us in the 60s – they appear rather magnificent, still soldiering along in their splendidly non-PC way, like some tribe that's been cut off from civilisation, suddenly discovered in the Amazonian jungle. And in a way they can get away with it, because Gibraltarians themselves are a mixture of British, Italian, Maltese and Portuguese and Genoese, with a strong Muslim, Hindu and Jewish contingent.

When I was there in the 60s, this society represented everything I hated. But now I look back on the scene with a kind of dippy sentimentality, because, whether it remains British or whether it's incorporated into some kind of Spanish rule, Gibraltarian life cannot last. American and British television is blared into every household – and it is very strange to watch *Have I Got News For You*, walk out and buy a beer with English pounds in the Prince of Wales pub, walk into the blazing sunshine, past Monsoon, the Body Shop and M&S, and then saunter through the frontier into Spain in a matter of minutes.

Gibraltar's Senior Citizens' Club, which announces on the door that 'Visiting Senior Citizens are Welcome' seems charming, rather than ridiculous, and even one of the newspapers, *VOX*, which has as its masthead: 'Established since 1956. For Law and Order without Fear or Favour', appears touching rather than threatening. News of the day may be that a derelict car is still derelict after five weeks.

A trip to the once-exotic Tangiers, however, is no longer nearly as exciting as it was in the 60s. The souk has been cleaned up. The men wear European clothes, and the women increasingly, too. The glamour has gone, along with the cockroaches.

Far better to stay in Gibraltar, visit the Barbary apes, go out with the dolphins and, in the evening, nip down for a G&T at La Bayuca restaurant, run by Johnnie and Tita, who've been on the go since 1964. The immensely glam old Johnnie is rumoured once to have had an affair with Ava Gardner, and you can see why. The walls are lined with photographs of Lew Hoad, the Duke of Edinburgh (admiral of the Gib yacht club), Jack Hawkins, Anthony Quayle, Deborah Kerr, Chris Chataway and Bill Cotton. After your third drink you're wondering whether the whole thing shouldn't be filmed in black and white, whether Fanny and Johnnie Craddock might suddenly pop out of the woodwork, whether you shouldn't really be discussing the merits of Honkers and KL and, a bottle of wine later, swearing that before you go home you'll jolly well buy a Union Jack, drape it from your home in London and damn the natives.

In the summer of 1968, the first Channel crossing by a car-carrying hovercraft was made; the *Princess Margaret* finally left service in 2000.

A CARRY-ON UP THE KHYBER, 1968

Heather Bolton remembers a trip to Pakistan in a van full of baby clothes.

Being stuck at Torkham, the Pakistani frontier, after a 6,000-mile journey in a ten-year-old Morris 1000 van, did not seem funny at the time. It made me wonder what on earth I was doing at the foot of the Khyber Pass in the first place.

It was 1968, and I was on my way to Lahore. The customs official, however, nearly made this an impossible dream: he was convinced we had made the entire journey in order to open a shop. I had met my friend Farooq, a Pakistani, in London two years earlier, and he had persuaded me that Lahore would be a great place to visit. He himself had been trying for about eight years to organise a trip back to his homeland.

The problem at the border had originated prior to our departure. Farooq's friends and acquaintances had arrived from all over London, all carrying parcels which they wished us to transport to their families at home. Many of these packages contained children's garments, in the same style but in a multitude of sizes. Looking back, I am not surprised that the official at the Khyber Pass was wary of our motive for going to Lahore.

After many hours of argument he eventually stamped our passports, but by that time it was dark. He leaned slowly back in his chair and said: 'Unfortunately there is tribal warfare in the vicinity, and it is not unknown for white people to be kidnapped and disappear.'

We were left with little alternative than to stay the night on the encampment. Farooq slept in a barracks, and as I was the only female I spent the night sleeping upright in the front of the van with an armed guard standing alongside. Those wretched parcels had caused further discomfort: they totally filled the space at the back, so that we had been obliged throughout the journey, when we had no other accommodation, to sleep upright in the front of the van.

Indeed, our journey had been riddled with such practical difficulties. For example, a windscreen wiper, flying off on an autobahn in Germany in driving rain, had further repercussions. Our only remaining one was transferred to the driver's side – and as the passenger I therefore got a very blurred view of the deserts of Iran.

But things got worse; a fan that Farooq had installed to cool the engine collected the dust and fired it at our faces as well as on to the bonnet. Farooq was able to see to drive only by keeping his wiper working nonstop. As I was not fortunate enough to have a wiper, I had to be content with eating the dust that also infiltrated my ears, nose and eyes.

In fact we got so dirty that we were refused refreshment at a desert rest-house. The landlady ordered us to wash in a nearby stagnant pond and then collapsed with laughter when she discovered that one of us was brown, the other white. She told us that she could never have guessed.

Eventually we arrived in Lahore and were taken into the bosom of Farooq's warm and loving family. Although middle class and well educated, descended from a long line of physicians, the family seemed very poor to me. The frugality of their home was at first a shock, but their hospitality quickly made up for it. Six beautiful children were being cared for by their two aunts, Farooq's sisters. The children's mother had died the year before, during the birth of the sixth, Anse.

Life in Lahore opened a door to a new dimension for me. Nothing could be hurried. Everything had its own pace. Conversations with Farooq's brother, the doctor, were totally unlike anything in the West. The tendency not to compartmentalise what was said, and not necessarily to compare it with direct experience, meant that there was an amazing freedom in our talk. It was almost as if ideas could be tossed around in time, seen from numerous angles.

Conversations like these would usually take place at dusk. The air would be heavy with the perfume of blossom. I felt such pathos that it was difficult not to weep. Children with brown eyes deeper than pools would listen quietly and attentively. Their ages ranged from twelve, to baby Anse. I am happy to say that today, more than thirty years later, I am still in touch with many of Farooq's family. Parting with them that summer, after a five-week stay, seemed grotesquely painful. I was to fly back, Farooq to return with the van.

On the way home I changed planes in Moscow, where the cold was shocking. As I stepped off, the wind whipped my cheeks – a cruel reminder of the love I had left in Pakistan.

In 1968, the sophisticated way to reach Pakistan was aboard a BOAC VC-10. The jet was another commercial failure for Britain.

THE GYPSIES OF GÜNZBERG, 1968

Duncan Reekie and his siblings practise the 'bombooshie' while his dad searches for a Bavarian head gasket.

Suddenly the motor began to falter and Dad swerved disparately off the autobahn and up an off ramp. Then the engine sputtered and died, but the road gave out to a steep incline, and so the Reekie family rolled down into the town of Günzberg, Bavaria in 1968.

We were holiday bound for the Federal People's Republic of Yugoslavia in a scruffy Renault camper van borrowed from my Aunt Pamela. We had no seat belts, no travel insurance and precious little money. 'I knew this would happen, John,' Mum cursed, but Dad reassured us in his eternally optimistic tone, and we believed him because he was our Dad.

My parents were – and still are – white middle-class socialists who, from a combination of utopian idealism and astute social service targeting, had adopted two black kids. My brother Stephen was mixed-race Caribbean/white aged ten, my sister Ella was mixed-race Asian/white aged seven. I was also seven and my sister, Katherine, was only four, but we were not adopted; we were the 'born' children, as Ella called us.

Things in the back of the van were not good. It was both boring and hazardous. We had to sit on treacherous vinyl cushions and if we hit a bumpy patch, the overhead cupboard doors would swing open and hit you on the head. To pass the time Stephen had been singing 'The Old Bamboo' from *Chitty Chitty Bang Bang* for the last ten miles. Katherine was crying and Ella and I were at the back window making

V-signs at the cars behind. We greeted the death of the van with enthusiasm and we especially loved freewheeling down the hill into the heart of the Fatherland.

It was dusk when we finally came to rest in a wooded lane on the outskirts of town. My Dad managed to coast the van off the road and pitch our tents and my Mum prepared our tea. For convenience and thrift she had brought along a vast supply of cash-and-carry dried meals; beef stroganoff or chicken supreme. You just added hot water to produce a beige magma that tasted of burned soap. What made this wonder-food all the more futuristic was that we ate it off turquoise plastic plates whose surface was so oily that it repelled food as if it were mercury.

Later, I lay under the stars in my green vinyl sleeping bag watching bats flutter over the van. My Dad was in the front seat listening to the World Service news by the light of a torch; the Russians had invaded Czechoslovakia. I stared into the night and thought about which would be the most lasting and useful superhero power: invisibility, teleportation or flight. Also, I thought about the Action Man I had mutilated and buried in the garden and I thought about the felt squares they had at school and how beautiful all the different colours of felt were.

In the morning we awoke to the sound of laughing children and splashing water for, by chance, we had camped almost opposite the Günzberg Municipal Lido. We grabbed our towels and costumes and Mum led us off to the pool, leaving Dad to repair the van. Mum bought our tickets at the foyer and then we passed through the steel turnstiles into the shining light of the Lido. Set in landscaped woodland of knolls and poplars was an immaculate modern glass and concrete complex built around a vast curved pool, which shimmered in the heat haze. There were diving boards, slides and fuming waterspouts. The beautiful youth of Günzberg flipped and flashed in the pool while across the lawns the adults sunbathed, picnicked and read their paperback novels.

It was heaven. We spent the next week as amphibious nymphs coursing through the elements. Every day, my Mum would set up camp amongst the trees and we would scurry down to the pool. Stephen was fearless, diving from the top board, his brown skin refracted in the deep end. Ella and me loved the slides, and we developed a series of elaborate and distinctive styles of descending, each with its own name. Our favourite was the 'bombooshie'. Katherine kept her water wings on and followed us with grim determination into the froth. When we were hungry there was a kiosk where we could buy lemonade and chips in plastic trays with a little wooden fork and a sachet of tomato sauce. They were expensive, but we were saving money on admission to the pool since, when the management heard about our break-down, they decided to let us in free.

Strangely, we seemed to fascinate the Bavarian bathers; the kids were just curious but the adults gazed at us with unrestrained delight or gave us incomprehensible words of friendly encouragement. In return we sniggered at their unfashionable costumes, their body hair and, most of all, the elaborate rubber swimming caps sported by the Günzberg ladies. These came in musty shades of lilac, salmon, jade and sky blue, patterned with swirls and dots, but the most fabulous had rubber flowers or tendrils, like the inside of an alien gland. Ella and I thought they were hysterical and we would follow their wearers about the pool giggling, the bemused reactions of our victims only made us more helpless with laughter.

Meanwhile, my Dad spent his time walking into town, phoning the bank and waiting for a new head gasket to arrive at the nearest Renault garage. He also made several new friends, deploying his technique of speaking loudly and amiably to foreigners in English. Hand extended, he would approach the hapless subject with a broad grin on his face and announce, 'Hello, John Reekie ...' But this actually worked. Towards the end of the week a young couple turned up at the van. They were reporters for the local newspaper and had come to investigate sightings of the first gypsies to visit Günzberg since the war. Instead they found a new friend and pen pal, John Reekie.

Later that evening, as we ate our beige stroganoff, Dad told us what he had learned about the town from his travels and encounters. Günzberg was the home of the Mengele family who owned the agricultural engineering company that dominated the town. Moreover, it had been the home of Dr Joseph Mengele, the infamous Nazi scientist who had experimented on children in Auschwitz. At the end of the war Mengele had fled back to Günzberg and hid there for a year before fleeing to South America. I asked my father what kind of things Mengele did to children and he said something about changing the colour of their eyes, which I didn't think was that bad.

The next day we became involved in a new and exciting activity at the pool. We discovered that the kiosk sold elasticised necklaces made of sweets, which you could wear and slowly nibble until only the string remained. We pestered Mum to buy us one each and wore them constantly. However, repeated immersion in the pool combined with the heat of the sun turned the necklace into sugary goo around our necks, which then attracted roving wasps. The only way to escape the wasps was to jump into the water – and so perpetuate the viscous circle. It never occurred to us to take the necklaces off.

Inevitably the new head gasket arrived and Dad fixed the van. Our last day at the pool seemed all the more perfect since we knew we would never return. The sun shone bright and high in the perfect blue sky. We hurled ourselves down the slides and somersaulted off the boards. We sat in the shallows and scowled. Why couldn't we stay longer? Why did everything always have to be so boring?

I queued up for the top diving board one last time. A week in the sun had turned my skin gold and my hair blond. A hand gripped my shoulder and I turned around. An old man with grey hair was staring down into my face. His face was lined with deep, dark creases and he was smiling, but there was something urgent about his eyes, about his grip. 'Deutsche?' he asked me. 'Deutsche?'

'What?' I replied. 'No speaken dee Deutsche.'

He smiled and drifted away, and I felt that somehow I had let him down and that something had been lost.

In 2004 a family of six could travel anywhere in Bavaria by train for a flat fare of €22 (£16) per day.

1970s

LIVING OFF THE LAND, 1970

A family pony-trekking trip in the Elan Valley was heavenly, and even camping was OK, says Victoria Summerley. But she drew the line at nettle soup.

When you live from hand to mouth, it is the food you remember most. And the food I remember most from our pony-trekking trip to Wales is the nettle soup my mother insisted on making when we ran out of money one cold, rainy night.

To take four children on a pony-trekking holiday is not an inexpensive undertaking. My mother decided to save money by spending only the first week under a conventional roof. For this, we stayed in a B&B in Rhayader, where there were hot baths, huge breakfasts and packed lunches supplied. The second week, the plan was to camp in a field nearby, close to the river Wye. By that time, the reasoning went, we would all be toughened up and scorn namby-pamby luxuries such as hot water.

My most vivid memory of the trekking was sitting in a miserable slouch on my Welsh Mountain pony in the never-ending rain. The trekkers fell into the usual horsy categories. There were the know-all fourteen-year-olds who seem to haunt most riding stables and develop intimate, possessive relationships with their ponies to make up for not having a boyfriend. They spent their whole time kicking their horses on, shrieking at each other and trying to chat up the trek leader.

At the other end of the scale were the non-riders, who were content to amble along, taking in the beauty of the Elan

Valley – the 'Lakeland of Wales' – and looked rather alarmed when anyone suggested a canter. I nearly fell off when my pony decided to roll in a peat bog and my little sister came off when she reached up to push away a branch as she waited to ford a stream. Unfortunately, the pony moved on, leaving my sister behind, hanging from the branch. She was saved by the trek leader, who came cantering back and swept her on to his saddle in the best Errol Flynn tradition. (All the fourteen-year-olds were terribly jealous.)

There's nothing like being on a horse to make you appreciate scenery. I've been back to the Elan Valley since, by car, and although the dams and reservoirs looked as majestic as ever (they provide Birmingham with its water supply) they seemed much more distant, more impersonal in a strange kind of way. I suppose walkers must have the same sort of feeling of connection with the land, but on a horse there's also the option of crossing it that much more quickly.

After paying for this part of the holiday, we didn't have much money left, so my mother made ends meet by drawing or painting the trekking ponies and flogging the results in one of the many pubs. (Our B&B was one of these – I seem to remember there were thirteen pubs altogether.) The idea was that the trekkers might be persuaded to part with a few pounds for a picture of 'their' pony as a souvenir. In fact, the pub landlords seemed even more enthusiastic about her work and two of the paintings were bought for twenty pounds each, which seemed an extraordinary amount. (My mother is an art-college graduate, but even so, we were impressed.)

Those were the fish-and-chip nights. But twenty pounds didn't go far, even in those days, with four children on your hands, particularly when one managed to lose a shoe in a peat bog and another wore right through her hand-me-down sandals. Clothes weren't so much of a problem: we all had tie-dyed T-shirts in orange, pink and yellow, which we were instructed to wear at all times so that we could be easily identified.

One night, it rained so hard that the Wye rose quite high, flooding the bottom of the field where we were camping and necessitating the hasty repitching of our tents. Somehow, in the melee, our evening meal was either trampled or spoiled. We had no food and no money, but there was an abundance of nettles, so my mother decided to make soup.

We children thought this was a totally despicable idea. For a start, we knew we'd have to gather the nettles and our field seemed to breed a particularly vicious variety. Second, we could predict with total accuracy, and did so at the tops of our voices, that we weren't going to like the results. Sure enough, about an hour later we sat in a sulky circle as what looked like bowls of green-grey algae were handed round. There was no salt, or pepper, or sour cream, or chicken stock, or anything else that might have made it palatable. 'You can't really be hungry if you don't want any,' my mother said firmly.

Then, like the Seventh Cavalry, like the Relief of Mafeking, like the sun breaking through a stormy sky, the two boys in the next tent came back from a fishing expedition on the Wye. They'd caught lots of trout, they told us, too much for the two of them to eat, so would we like some? Would we like some? Do tents leak when it rains?

They were about seventeen or eighteen and we hadn't really talked to them before, because they seemed very grown-up, and thus irrelevant, to us. My mother approved of them because they were 'nice boys' (i.e. they had good manners and posh accents). But from then on, they might as well have been young gods as far as we were concerned.

We gazed at them adoringly, salivating while they fried what seemed like an endless supply of trout on a little pan over a Calor Gas stove. It was sublime, with that leap-in-the-mouth effect that you only get from really fresh food. I've never had anything since, not at the Ivy or Nobu or any other smart restaurant, that tasted as good as that trout. And I've never since eaten nettles.

On 22 January 1970, the first commercial flight of the Boeing 747 took place, on Pan Am from New York Kennedy to London Heathrow. The flight arrived three hours late due to technical problems, and the onward leg to Frankfurt was cancelled because of bad weather in Germany.

A RACE UNLIKE OURSELVES, 1970

Virginia Ironside found that 'troot' was stranger than fiction in the land of babushkas and smuggled bananas.

Visiting Moscow in 1970 was like paying a visit to one of those far-away planets in *Star Wars*. It wasn't just that the architecture was so different from anything I had seen before – the golden-topped onion domes of the Kremlin, the wedding-cake architecture of Stalin's seven mammoth buildings constructed by German prisoner-slaves – no, the people themselves were a race unlike ourselves.

On the one hand, there were the moody, drunken, Raskolnikov-style students – threadbare, starved, reading uncut books by candlelight, glimpsed through curtainless windows along dark streets. And the old men who played dominoes in the park, as they must have done for centuries. And peasant women in headscarves, wearing men's jackets over long, spotted skirts. On the other hand, there were the party faithfuls who appeared to put have put aside any thoughts of humanity in their devotion to Lenin.

In those days, it was exceptionally difficult to go to Russia except on an Intourist tour, and for £180, cheap even then, we took a two-week all-in tour. Visas were hard to get and because I was a journalist and my paper had apparently been unsympathetic in its coverage of a cholera epidemic, we had to wait for hours under an enormous portrait of Lenin in the Soviet embassy until a huge, scarred Russian official could be persuaded that my journalism was more of the light-hearted, television review, advice-to-teenagers style than that of subversive investigation.

Along with a few Marxist tracts, I was handed a copy of the *Soviet Weekly*, which contained an implausible article about the abundance of fine shoes in Russia. It also proclaimed: 'Socialist justice believes in man's fundamental rights.'

When I returned from Russia, I rang to ask whether I could write a piece about my trip. 'Of course,' came the thick, flat tones of the official, 'but only if you write the troot.' I decided that, if I ever wanted to visit again, it would be best to remain silent.

Even the Aeroflot plane was extraordinary, a mixture of Edwardian baroque and 60s functionalism jammed awkwardly together, the loo a Jules Verne pantomime with a huge, voluptuous marble sink and stained wooden doors. Lunch was an apple, some cheese and corned beef, and three marzipan sweets in the shape of fruits.

Once in the arrivals hall of Moscow Airport, with its epically high ceiling decorated with frescoes of workers and sheaves of corn, we were told we had to divest ourselves of any subversive magazines – copies of *Playboy* were immediately confiscated by giggling customs officials – and also any fruit we had brought. Panicked by reports of shortages, old ladies' zipper bags, which I imagined to be full of crochet and books by Agatha Christie, were opened to reveal piles of apples, pears and bananas. The customs office began to look like an orchard, and soon the entire tour was stuffing themselves with apples in order to finish them up as quickly as possible. We had been asked to take two packets of Polyfilla for a English correspondent we knew in Moscow – he had cockroaches in his bathroom – and the stuff evinced suspicious amazement from the guards.

We stayed in a terrible hotel, each floor of which was guarded by a Russian giantess who kept the keys. She would log us in whenever we left or returned and, like everyone else in Moscow, had an enormous briefcase in which to cram her endless notes and reports. The food was inedible, there were no plugs in the sinks – plugs having been forgotten that year in the list of economic needs – and when our guide, Ivan ('My name is Ivan the Terrible, so we will have a terrible time') cracked jokes about going for walks in Siberia, all we could do was giggle nervously.

Our tour was full of old believers from England who backed Stalin to the hilt, and whose eyes sparkled at every crazy statistic we were given. One, from Yorkshire, declared: 'The White Sea canal was not built by slave labour, as the propaganda in the West claimed. It was a most enlightened penal experiment.'

Despite the obvious poverty, the queues, the lack of goods in the shops apart from the occasional delivery of cabbage, bread or sausage, and the rusting, bolted churches outside which old babushkas knelt on the pavements and prayed, crossing themselves pathetically, there was a feeling of wild certainty about the place. Everyone knew they were right. We were the decadent ones.

There was something moving and uplifting about seeing, as we did, a bus driver reading Zhukov's memoirs during his stopping-points; about walking through the crazily ornate metro system and passing miles and miles of people selling books, books, and more books to information-hungry customers. The streets were wide and carless, except for the huge state lorries that rumbled through. Lenin's tomb – complete with goose-stepping guards and soldiers with bayonets guarding the dimly lit body inside, with its queue of country-dwellers (come up to see him as a treat) running round the square – was a phenomenon that both sickened and excited us. It was so peculiar.

Then there was the Exhibition of Economic Achievements, all Third-Reich classical architecture with CCCP and star motifs in relief everywhere – acres of land devoted to areas such as the Gold Head of Wheat Fountain, or the Concentrated Fodder-Making Pavilion, a vast Grecian temple. Our fat, blonde, sweet-faced guide droned on and on: 'Our country's eighth satellite – over there – had transmission mechanism independent of propulsion unit so directional pull was . . . Every fifth book in the world is published in Moscow . . . Moscow is the sixth biggest city in the world . . . In Moscow there are 26 doctors for every 100,000 people . . . On your left is a hotel built for businessmen coming to Moscow . . . On your right you will get a view of the stadium, grey in colour, which seats 100,000 people . . .' Tears poured down her face as she showed us a statue of Lenin.

A subversive in our group asked: 'Could a Ukrainian nationalist theoretically be nominated to the Supreme Soviet?'

'A what?'

'A Ukrainian nationalist.'

'There are no nationalists in Ukraine. No one would want to elect one.'

'But could one be elected, given the non-party seats that are set aside?'

'No one would want to be a Ukrainian nationalist. No one wants to secede from the Soviet Union.'

Now, all has changed. If it was dismal then, at least it had faith in something. On my most recent visit, Moscow had turned into a vast, horrible supermarket. Western music blared out everywhere. Traffic jams were the norm. The bookstores were gone; statues of Lenin were to be found only in the Sunday tourist market, for inflated prices. The posters of hammers and sickles were being sold as Soviet kitsch for tourists. Gum, the huge department store, was full of Calvin Klein, the Body Shop, Next and Kookai. Restaurants had sprung up, but they could be restaurants anywhere. The goose-stepping soldiers guarding Lenin's tomb had vanished, and the soldiers inside did not stick guns in your face as you passed. The churches were refurbished, crumbling buildings had been lovingly restored. Gypsy beggars lined the underground, clutching white-faced children. Moscow could have been any other European city, drenched with consumerism and capitalism.

On 12 September 1970, in a Jordanian desert, three hijacked aircraft – a BOAC VC-10, a TWA Boeing 707 and a Swissair DC-8 – were blown up by Palestinians after the passengers and crew had been released.

NO SEX, NO DRUGS – JUST ROCK, 1971

In '71, everybody staged festivals. So no one thought it strange that Clacton Round Table should join the rock bandwagon, as Simon Calder recalls.

In summer 2002 in Hyde Park, 150,000 people were a quarter-century too late. They paid £8 each for eight hours of rock music. Twenty-five years earlier they could have got much more for less. At the start of 1971, I queued all night outside the Big Apple in Brighton and paid 18 shillings (90p) to see the Rolling Stones. And as the year aged, the music blossomed. The summer of 1971 was when travel and British rock music converged for a glorious five-month binge of outdoor gigs.

It was the year the Glastonbury Festival began, with a promise from the organisers that 'We are tapping the Universe'. Unfortunately it was the warning from the welfare charity Release that: 'There are no facilities. At the moment there is one toilet and half a trench dug. No water supplies, nothing', which persuaded my parents this would be a gig too far. But from Crystal Palace to the Oval, via Hyde Park and Clacton, that summer seemed miraculous for the young traveller in search of music.

Before you began to hitch around southern England from one muddy field to the next, you had to look the part. Fortunately, this was a simple matter of not cutting your hair for six months, and buying accoutrements by mail order: maroon Loon Pants, 28-inch flare, £2.85; self-assembly fringed moccasins, £5.97; *Warlock of Love* (an anthology of poetry by Marc Bolan), 75p. Then the summer began.

* * *

May: the most underrated park in the capital is the elaborate confection of Crystal Palace. An Eiffel-esque television transmitter exclaims that this is the highest point in London. Beside it, a ghostly space the size of several football fields lies bereft of anything more than a few scruffy weeds. Yet this was the site of the Crystal Palace, a glass structure that brought the hopes and designs of the Victorian world to London SE19. The venue for the Great Exhibition was destroyed by fire in 1936, and since then the grounds have been abandoned to seed.

A scruffy weed myself, I travelled to the Pink Floyd concert in ignorance of the significance of the site. With a loaf of sliced white bread, and a tin of Spam that would become a motif for the summer, I followed the cloud of joss-stick smoke emitting from be-flared hippies gathered around the giant concrete shell that served as a stage.

Beneath a threatening sky that sometimes darkened to the colour of black vinyl, we squeezed like Japanese commuters into an arena several sizes too small for the 15,000 crowd. Unwilling and unable to move, we waited with bursting bladders to find if Pink Floyd would close with 'Atom Heart Mother' or 'Set the Controls for the Heart of the Sun'. It was the latter.

June: the month when I went nowhere more exotic than the isolation ward of Crawley Hospital was also the most mobilising. A dose of teenage meningitis kept me horizontal while I unravelled a whole new world from the pages of a brand-new book. My parents, no doubt anxious to offload one of their surplus young for the summer, gave me the very first edition of the *Hitchhikers' Guide to Europe* as a get-well present. Nowadays, Traveller's-Rough-Survival-Guides are ten-a-nation. But in the summer of '71, the idea that you could spend £1.25 on book subtitled 'How to see Europe by the skin of your teeth' was as revolutionary as the five-track single released that month by Jethro Tull, 'Life is a Long Song'.

July: Liz Haywood was training to be a teacher in Bognor Regis. My good fortune in having two indulgent older sisters, with car-owning friends, meant I was taken to gigs that should have been well beyond my dreams. While Van Der Graaf Generator laboured through a particularly dreary set one night at Bognor College, I got talking to Liz. Though we shared nothing more intimate than a couple of inmate-thin roll-ups (Old Holborn, blue Rizlas), we vowed to meet again. And 3 July was supposed to be the day. With 48 hours to go, she cancelled, no doubt because of a better offer – it would not need to be much of an offer to improve upon spending a Saturday with a youth, four years her junior, enduring possibly the loudest and certainly the worst rock'n'roll band in the world.

Grand Funk Railroad had taken out full-page ads in the music press thanking the Department of the Environment for permission to stage the free concert. In retrospect, the minister responsible, Peter Walker, should have resigned. Mark, Don and Mel comprised a kind of Satanic version of Peter, Paul and Mary. At the time Michael Watts, later a colleague at the *Independent*, described them in *Melody Maker* as 'shallow, dull, trite and mediocre'. After a two-hour set, without Liz Haywood for company, I regarded his review as too kind. If there is any justice in the music business, the trio will nowadays be pumping gas somewhere towards the rough end of New Jersey.

Humble Pie provided admirable support, but the biggest cheer of the afternoon was when the DJ played 'Lola' by the

Kinks. The idea of going to a club in old Soho with someone who 'walked like a women but talked like a man' was racy talk in a nation only just mastering decimal currency.

August: If you aim for Clacton but stop seven miles short, you will find yourself in the middle of a field. Welcome to Weeley.

In '71, everyone was holding festivals. So no one thought it strange that Clacton Round Table should climb aboard the rock bandwagon and promote three days of the best of British music in aid of local charities. The Weeley Festival of Progressive Rock was a kind of village fete gone ballistic.

Vic Speck was the unlikely name behind this event. He persuaded T Rex and Lindisfarne, Rod Stewart and Status Quo to turn up at a venue that had no track record and has not been used for anything other than pasture ever since the event. Most of the 140,000 audience arrived by train, at a tiny station straight out of *The Railway Children*. For three days and nights we (and, unhappily, the Spam) sweated through the hottest Bank Holiday for years, as a procession of bands and 4,000 watts of Marshall PA tore through the calm, still air of Constable country.

Barclay James Harvest turned up for their set with a 45-piece orchestra, but most of the musicians were drowned out by the scream of sirens belonging to the Essex fire brigade. Enterprising festival-goers had constructed straw igloos from bales left in the fields by farmers. Add hot, dry weather, a joss stick and a joint or two and you have the ideal ingredients for a succession of fires. No one was hurt, which was sadly not the case during the T Rex set. Marc Bolan's band followed – or rather failed to follow – Rod Stewart and the Faces. A shower of bottles and cans rained down upon the stage.

* * *

September: 'Less Music by Dead Guys' promises Coast 97.3, a North Carolina radio station. But the show in Hyde Park in 2002 demonstrated how the music of '71 has endured. In May 1971, the Who released their best album, *Who's Next*. Three decades on, the surviving members of the band tackled 'Won't Get Fooled Again' less frantically than they did at the Oval on 18 September 1971.

New York's concert in aid of the people of the newly independent Bangladesh took place at Madison Square Garden and featured George Harrison and Bob Dylan. Ours was beneath a gasometer in south London, at the home of Surrey County Cricket Club. The tender turf of the Oval was covered in rope matting in order that 35,000 fans could pay £1.25 each to see Emerson, Lake and Palmer warm up the crowd for the Who, at the Vauxhall end. The previous summer, Jimi Hendrix had set the trend for guitar destruction by smashing his Stratocaster at the Isle of Wight festival. After 'windmilling' (rotating the plectrum-wielding arm wildly) his way through 'Won't Get Fooled Again', Pete Townshend doused his bloody hand in a mug of whisky to anaesthetise it. Then he set about destroying his brand-new Gibson and hurling the wreckage into the crowd. Finally the soon-to-be-late Keith Moon chose to exit the stage by the novel method of trampling through his drum kit – a final violent cadence to the closest Britain ever came to a summer of love.

Melody Maker headlines that summer:
  Peel hits at BBC drugs ban
  At last: Radio 1 goes heavy
  Folk on Radio 1: what's going on?
  T Rex: the shine has worn off
  Morrison leaves $3 million

Jethro Tull in US riots – 'Like World War Three'
Common Market pop: we say NON!
Sarstedt: where did he go to?
Elvis heading for UK
Elton to play for Kennedys
Elton bores 'em at the Palace
BB King, Lennon to jam?
Harrison and Moon join Beach Boys

On 4 February 1971, Rolls-Royce went bankrupt.

THE AMAZING TECHNICOLOR SIDEWALK, 1971

New York's busy streets and the shock of modern art plunged Russell Gould, then a twelve-year-old schoolboy from the Midlands, into hairy adolescence. And a rather nice new Junior High School uniform.

Stansted didn't seem like an airport; it was more like a World War II airfield, with a shed for a terminal and a single runway. But it was where the Gould family was to make their embarkation for the New World in the summer of 1971. My parents, brother and I were off to the United States. We would stay in New York City, and then go upstate to Ithaca, where my father, for six months, would be a Visiting Professor at Cornell University and I would attend DeWitt Junior High School. I tried to envisage how it would be different from my boys-only school in the Midlands, which was strict about its monochrome uniform of black blazer and trousers and black-and-white tie on crisp white shirt. Would we play football? Did they have cricket? Moreover, what would the teachers be like? My grammar school masters were feared and respected – the place had only abolished caning a few years earlier. Surely they couldn't be stricter than that?

The England we were leaving behind was a drab place of Harold Wilson, Ted Heath, Mother's Pride and *Opportunity Knocks*. Only the colour and excitement of *On The Buses*, the occasional *Carry On* film and newspaper stories about the skinhead 'menace' punctuated routine life.

The aircraft we boarded was an aging chartered plane about one-third full, and promised to be interminably boring for a twelve-year-old boy. In-flight entertainment had yet to be invented; I had to be grateful that I had grabbed a copy of *Look-In* at the newsagents before boarding. We were attended to by curiously robotic air stewardesses in turquoise uniforms who brought plastic trays of inedible food, their heavy make-up becoming increasingly congealed over the course of the journey.

I was on my way to a Technicolor dreamland I had only seen on black-and-white television. The place where Ernie Bilko, Lucille Ball and Rowan and Martin endlessly wise-cracked and where the police, whom everyone called cops, carried guns. America was the land of hippies, Charles Manson, Andy Warhol, Elvis Presley, crew-cut astronauts and the US Presidents whose faces I knew from television news: Kennedy, Johnson and Nixon. This America was, in my mind, indelibly connected with the imported comic books I read at the time – not so much the bizarre heroes and villains, but the ads they carried for baseball mitts (whatever those were), X-ray specs and bubble gum. There was a curious magic in the abbreviations of the states to which one would send off for such novelties – TX, MN, CA – and the mysterious zip codes, which I could never fill in. There was also a place called Vietnam, somehow connected with America, but my young brain could not understand how. I knew what I was interested in: guitars, T Rex and Alice Cooper. Girls, drugs and politics did not yet figure.

On arrival, we stayed in an expensive hotel on Fifth Avenue whose long, carpeted corridors were eerily silent. The door of each room had a series of impressively robust locks but sleep was not easy, as the noise of the traffic and the shrieking sirens from the streets below was inescapable and constant. And so as not to be bathed in sweat throughout the night, the air conditioning was kept constantly on. By day, the New York summer heat was oppressive and impossible. The sidewalks were crowded with people moving at a frantic pace. Everyone was drenched in sweat as the temperature passed 100 degrees. No matter how much I drank, I was constantly thirsty.

Steam hissed from sidewalks spotted with used syringes, and my mother would pull me away sharply whenever my curiosity caused me to linger at some evidence of aberrant dereliction or immorality, such the garishly dressed transvestites in the night-time mayhem of Times Square, or the beggars nested in doorways, crying out for spare change. Both the US Army recruitment building and the guns, ammo and knife shop that faced Times Square were doing brisk business.

One afternoon, while walking with my parents – I was considered far too young to be allowed out on the streets by myself – across the road I heard a sudden percussive shot; turning towards the direction of the gunfire I could make out a bloodied man lying on the ground. This was both shocking and exciting. I couldn't imagine this happening in my home town in England, where arguments in the street over football or women were settled at worst with boots, fists and bottles.

On the hottest day of August a generous relative took my brother and myself to an Edward Kienholz retrospective at the Whitney Museum of American Art. I was stunned by a disturbing installation piece called *The Wait*, in which an ancient woman composed of brown rags, jars and sticks, with a framed portrait for a head, sits on a sepia chair amid the decaying relics of her life. The Whitney was amazing. I had previously only seen modern art in books at my local library and here, before my eyes, were original Jasper Johns, Lichtensteins and Pollocks. It was a long way from Stewpot's request page in *Look-In*, and I suddenly felt something fundamental was shifting. Without a single word, I had a realisation that there was a whole world of 'stuff' out there waiting for me to seek it out.

A couple of days later, walking away from Greenwich Village, I was told that we were near Warhol's current Factory, and I dragged my family to look at the nondescript building in Union Square, which had an American flag flying outside. I wish I had dared to ring the bell and say hello to Andy.

Having spent about a month in New York City we departed JFK airport on a Mohawk Air flight to Ithaca, in upstate NY – a terrifying ride in what seemed like a 1940s bomber plane. Ithaca was a small university town, nothing like New York City, and it felt that I was being cruelly snatched from my new life as a wannabe art critic in the big city to be deposited into small-town, Douglas Sirk America. My father drove a huge rented car to the huge rented house. The street where we were to live had a white picket fence. We were one house among many big houses with clean front porches, neighbours who wanted to be our buddies, and well-behaved kids. The television set in the 'den' was enormous and was the first colour TV I had ever seen. But watching it for the first time made me nauseous. I thought American television was clearly insane. It consisted of a hundred channels of ceaseless hysterical mayhem, broken up only by ads that were clever and addictive.

When I was bought my new school clothes from JC Penney, I expected having to try on something similar to my grammar school uniform. Instead I was presented with fantastic blue and red striped trousers like Marc Bolan had worn on *Top Of The Pops*. There were brightly coloured T-shirts and lace-up sneakers that I immediately wanted to run and climb trees in, unlike the sad British plimsoles, with their elasticated tops that made anyone who wore them look institutionalised. Once I had got my new kit, I was incredibly excited at the prospect of going to DeWitt Junior High School. No battered wooden desks, grim Victorian class-rooms or prison-style toilets there. The place had only just been built and was an ultra-modern steel, concrete and glass construction. Elements of the classic 1950s American school remained, however; the yellow bus that took me from my street to the school, the lockers, the ubiquitous Stars and Stripes, the gym with its basketball hoops and the vaguely frightening nuclear bomb shelter signs. I was delighted to find that the school had a liberal atmosphere; among its few rules was that the bringing of guns and narcotics into the school were forbidden. Every morning the Principal read the Pledge of Allegiance over the public address system while the whole school stood and mumbled along with him.

The unironically named school 'students' were a mixed bunch, from all races and classes. I liked being in the company of sullen, long-haired, would-be hippie adolescents and looked forward to being one soon myself. The teachers turned a blind eye to the cigarettes and pot being smoked in the toilets. From the age of twelve, boys and girls 'dated'. There were a few Black (in those days, always with a capital B) kids, who could be seen behind the glass walls at their Black Studies class, looking serious. With their 'Free Angela Davis' T-shirts and Black Power fist badges, they were prematurely political and seemed supremely cool.

The schoolwork seemed ridiculously easy and I had a lot of free time to read in the library, or just hang around doing nothing, thinking about art. My hair grew beyond my ears for the first time and I bought a portable cassette recorder – an unheard-of luxury in England. I made some friends who imitated how I spoke – being English was 'cool'. In biology class I very much enjoyed dissecting a foetal pig, placing its organs in separately labelled jars filled with formaldehyde. An interesting and unpatriotic classroom experiment involved putting some human teeth into a bottle of Coca-Cola and examining them the next day, by which time the teeth had mysteriously dissolved.

I longed to stay in New York for my teen years and become a student at Cornell University, where my father was teaching. The male students were bearded, denim-clad, friendly freaks and the women were beautiful flower-children in flared trousers and ponchos. All, however, had not been love and peace at Cornell. A few years before, there had been a shoot-out between some Black Panther students and the Sheriff's Department, and the bullet holes in the administration building were still visible. But I thought that made it even cooler.

In the evenings after school I would sit in my bedroom reading Beat literature that belonged to the son of the family whose house we were renting, and listening to Cream and Tiny Tim records on a tinny stereo. Downstairs my mother, being a 1970s mother, would be cooking or cleaning in the opulent American kitchen with its superfluity of gadgets. My father would be reading, preparing a lecture for the following day or watching the CBS news. Fall was under way, and throughout the night I heard spooky, echoing foghorns from boats on the nearby Cayuga River, and didn't want to be landlocked in the Midlands ever again.

But I knew this existence was temporary and that a former life of conformity and discipline awaited me in a bleak English town. I had seen a brasher, brighter world and lived, tantalisingly briefly, a different life. Something inside me had grown to expect something more than the conservative and drab England of the early 1970s. I now hated, with an angry and bitter loathing, the provincial dullness to which I would have to return. Years later, recognising the streets and people of 1970s New York on the cinema screen in *Trash* and *Taxi Driver*, I was filled with an incredible nostalgia. When I visited New York again in the 1980s the city had changed; it was cleaner, safer and more sanitised. But the Warhol silk-screens and Oldenburg drawings in the Whitney Museum were exactly the same.

In 1971, the cheap way to reach America was to join an 'affinity group charter'. First you had to join an invariably spurious association, such as the Scunthorpe Pigeon Fanciers' Club, then swear that you were a genuine member, in order to qualify for a flight at around half the prevailing scheduled fare.

STARVATION ON THE ORIENT EXPRESS, 1972

The world's most famous train has regained some of its glamour in recent years. But, thirty years ago, Anthony Lambert found his journey far from luxurious.

I wasn't expecting a palace on wheels when I decided to make my first journey across Europe by rail. I had chosen to travel on the most famous train of all, retracing its original route through Eastern Europe to Istanbul. But nothing had prepared me for quite how low the Orient Express had sunk in those twilight years, before the name and reputation of the train created by the Belgian Georges Nagelmackers were resurrected by James Sherwood in the 1980s. Otherwise I might have taken along some provisions.

The only hint of austerity as I made for Victoria station to join the overnight train–ferry service from London to Paris was the stillness of the streets on a June Sunday evening; consumerism had yet to make the Sabbath like any other day. Decadent bohemianism was being celebrated in the newly opened film musical *Cabaret*, soon to rival *The Godfather* at the box office, Ceylon had just gained independence to become Sri Lanka, and 'Vincent' by Don McLean was No. 1 in the charts.

The night ferry was a slow but civilised way to travel to Paris; even on a Sunday evening, orders for dinner were taken in the restaurant car as we slipped past the still-functioning, floodlit power station at Battersea. Our royal-blue wagons-lits sleeping cars were comfortable, if lacking style, but few slept through the shunting operations at Dover or the shackling of the coaches to the deck of the ship for the Channel crossing to Dunkirk.

Even Paris, albeit on a day of rain, seemed prosaic compared to the expectation of a journey to the gateway of Asia. The Orient Express left at 10.45 p.m. from Gare de l'Est, the same Paris station from which the first one had departed on 4 October 1883. As I wandered along the platform, it was impossible not to think of all the scenes in films enlivened by the drama of the trans-European express, from the adaptation of Graham Greene's *Stamboul Train*, and *The Lady Vanishes* to Agatha Christie's thriller inspired by her journeys on the famous train to her husband's archaeological digs in the Middle East.

There is something about overnight trains that lends an air of mystery and enchantment to travel – watching vignettes of other lives pass by the open window while catching the cooling breeze. Snatching sleep in a couchette or upright seat certainly takes the edge off the romance, but a night between crisp linen as hundreds of miles pass underneath your bed makes air travel seem squalid. To wake having no idea where you are, or even what country you are in, until architecture or the first station provides a clue, is a rare experience.

Certainty came with my first sight of Europe's tallest cathedral tower as the train entered Ulm beside the young Danube and the first of many steam locomotives hissed past. Breakfast appeared on a plastic tray at the compartment door just before Munich, where the first exchange of diplomatic bags took place through an open window. French *couriers diplomatiques* and British King's Messengers were frequent users of the Orient Express from the late 19th century, delivering documents for embassies and consulates along the route.

After reversing at Munich's terminus, the train climbed through the Bavarian Alps and the finest landscapes of the journey before crossing the Austrian border to reach Salzburg. As a portent of things to come, the restaurant car was detached at Vienna. Surely it would be replaced at Budapest? Although there was no hedge of barbed wire at the Austro-Hungarian border, there were watchtowers and soldiers standing beside the track with guard dogs the entire length of the train. As part of the border formalities, an interior coach panel was removed, presumably in a search for contraband. Perhaps I'd read too many Cold War thrillers, but there was a distinct chill about my first encounter with Soviet bloc border officials, as though it was forbidden to smile on duty. I set myself the challenge of extracting at least a minor twitch of the lips before Turkey, but never succeeded.

No dining car materialised at Budapest, and the trolley on board stocked only greasy salami rolls, so procurement of anything better required a rapid sprint to the buffet or a platform trolley at longer station stops. Romanian immigration and customs officials thought it fun to work from opposite ends of the train, so that sleep would be interrupted twice. I woke at Copsa Mica to witness what uncontrolled pollution can do to the colour of grass and trees, a sight soon redeemed by the medieval town of Sighisoara and the climb through the beech woods of Transylvania to Brasov.

At Bucharest I broke my journey to take the train across flat country to the Black Sea at Constanta. Until the completion of the railway through Bulgaria in 1889, all Orient Express passengers had to embark on a 27-hour sea passage to Istanbul. Back in Bucharest, I fell in with two local medical students while waiting for the train south. The worst excesses of Ceausescu's megalomania were still to come, but the students were already outspoken in their resentment of the regime's restrictions. Their flared trousers had been bought from tourists.

It was dark for the last crossing of the Danube at Giurgiu in Bulgaria. By dawn, white pencil-shaped minarets heralded the approach to Istanbul along the Sea of Marmara and beneath the walls of the Topkapi Palace to Sirkeci station. For someone just out of school, the ancient city straddling Europe on one side and and Asia on the other seemed a fabulously exotic place, an appropriate destination for a train that has twice cost a king's ransom to make it fit for royalty.

More than thirty years have passed since my youthful adventure and I am about to make the same journey on the Orient Express, forsaking its principal service to Venice for an annual retracing of the late 19th-century route to the Bosphorus; I have been assured that, this time, no platform sprints will be required.

In the summer of 1972, the Inter-Rail card was introduced. It allowed students unlimited travel on the railways of Europe, at £28.50 for one month.

THE BALKANS BY BEDFORD, 1972

A new motor caravan provided the perfect excuse for Victoria Summerley, her mum, family, and even lodgers to go on a Very Long Trip. Just don't mention Belgium.

In the summer of 1972, my mother bought a new motor caravan. It was a Bedford and I can't remember what model it was, but it looked like a pale-yellow ice-cream van. Up until then, we'd had to make do with second-hand VW camper vans and even, at one point, an old ambulance, so this truly thrilling acquisition had to be marked in some way. We decided to go on the biggest adventure of our lives. We would go not to Wales, or the New Forest, or Scotland, or France, or any of our usual camping grounds, but A Long Way. We would go to Greece and back.

Into the Bedford piled my mother, us four children and four of my mother's lodgers, wedged in among cans of beans, and camping kit, all of which had very hard edges. Two of the lodgers were hitching a lift as far as Ljubljana and Zagreb to visit relatives, while the other two were along for the ride.

The first part of the journey passed in a flash. One minute we were on the ferry and the next minute, or so it seemed, we were whizzing through the Alps before pitching camp at Genoa. My most vivid memory of the birthplace of Christopher Columbus was that Italian drivers don't stop at zebra crossings and I was nearly knocked down as I timidly ventured across the road to the beach.

We changed our minds about Italy's motoring madness, however, when the brand-new Bedford broke down near Bologna, after a day or so of strange behaviour. The

Bolognese mechanics were a marked contrast to their British equivalent. There were no sharp intakes of breath or shakes of the head. Instead, they almost cooed over the engine and crowded round to have a look at this strange British vehicle. We children had our cheeks pinched and the van must have got the automotive version of a pat on the head too, because it ran like a dream from then on. (Until my mother took it in for its next service back home in London, in fact.)

I don't think we were particularly blasé children, but the glories of Italy seemed somehow predictable. It was fun to see the Leaning Tower of Pisa (so small and squat compared to what we'd imagined) and the paintings in the Uffizi in Florence and St Mark's Square in Venice were dutifully admired. But this was culture and we felt we knew about all that. What we wanted was adventure. It was only when we crossed from friendly Italy, familiar from art books and documentaries, into what was then Tito's Yugoslavia that we really felt the exciting bit had begun. I can remember eating breakfast in a cafe in Split – croissants with plum jam – and thinking: 'This is really travelling.' I've liked plum jam ever since.

We journeyed on down the Dalmatian coast and spent a few days in Dubrovnik, taking in some sun, sea and sand. I listened to the polyglot chitchat on the beach around me and felt very smug when, thanks to my rudimentary French, I managed to tune in to the conversation of the family next to us. '*Pourquoi?*' their toddler was whining. '*Parce que!*' his mother snapped back. At fifteen, I felt like a true cosmopolitan.

In fact, I was the family scaredy-cat: the last to learn to swim, the last to ride a bike, positively the last ever to want to do anything that involved any kind of physical risk. But perhaps my new idea of myself as a citizen of the world had given me courage, because that afternoon I climbed into our little rubber dinghy and paddled myself about a mile out to sea to a little island that lay in the bay. The rest of the family were only half as astonished as I was myself.

From Dubrovnik, we journeyed inland, via Skopje – where I was amazed to see live chickens on sale in the market – skirting Albania. We passed the border, with a rank of grim, grey military-looking lorries parked as if deliberately to obscure any possible glimpse of Enver Hoxha's inscrutable state. We must have passed, I now realise, through Kosovo, although it is only since the Balkan civil wars that the name holds any resonance. But even as a teenager, I was astonished by the cultural changes as we drove on through the mountains.

The resorts of Croatia had seemed just like those of any other European resorts; the local teenage girls with enviable tans and tiny bikinis. Further south, the atmosphere was much more Eastern European, with horse-drawn carts taking families to market along roads that were fringed by fields of maize and vines. In the mountains of Macedonia, we saw women sitting by the side of the road in Muslim dress, while the road signs were now in Cyrillic as well as the Roman alphabet. It seemed a very strange mix of cultures; exotic, almost, to our untravelled eyes.

One night we camped by the side of the road, one of an unending series of hairpin bends. It was so hot, we just unrolled our groundsheets, laid sleeping bags on top of them and went straight to sleep. I awoke to the sounds of bells. For a minute, I couldn't think where I was, then something trod on my face. It was a herd of goats, led by a boy goatherd, who shrieked with laughter as he disentangled us from his charges.

On and on we went, down through Greece, via hot, dusty Athens and the obligatory Parthenon. At Delphi, we found the loud voices of Americans rather than the hoarse whisper of the Pythoness and the sighing of the wind in the pines. If Yugoslavia was a revelation, Delphi was a disappointment. But on the coast at Itea, then a quiet little village, we found a beach where I tried snorkelling for the first time. We even caught an octopus, a small one, which we decided to cook for supper.

A friendly local fisherman, watching our attempts to thwart its tentacular escape from our bucket, told us that we had to scrub it against the rocks to get rid of the slime, then turn its head inside out to kill it. He spoke very good English and his instructions were easy to understand. Nevertheless, we decided to throw the octopus back. But we accepted the fisherman's offer of a night-fishing trip in his boat that evening, powered by an outboard motor and with a lamp hanging from the stern to attract the fish. After about an hour, we had enough for a midnight feast, cooked over a driftwood fire on the beach.

Our route home, heading north via Belgrade, Salzburg and Munich, was punctuated by the interminable flash-flash of electric storms. By the time we got to Belgium, to visit the altarpiece at Ghent, it was pouring with rain and our long, hot summer on the road was nearly at an end. One of the lodgers and I asked in a local café if we could use the loo. A waiter told us it would be all right, but when we came out, the owner of the café started shouting at us, ranting about England letting Belgium down during the Second World War. Obviously unhinged, she finished by slapping my face.

I've often been back to Greece. Slobodan Milosevic made travelling in southern Yugoslavia impossible while he attempted to rid it of the very ethnic diversity that had so fascinated us. But it was more than thirty years before I could even contemplate the idea of going back to Belgium.

In 1972, the 'Clunk–Click' campaign was introduced in a bid to persuade motorists to use seat belts; belts were required to be fitted in newer cars, but there was no legal requirement to use them.

FLAMES OF PASSION IN THE DAYS OF FRANCO, 1972

Liz Nash hitched round Spain with a friend, fending off unwanted amorous advances.

My politically right-on friends warned me off Spain while Franco remained in power. Endorsing Fascism, they said. I was stung, but took no notice. Sue and I landed in Barcelona at dawn, or dusk, I forget, and gasped at the flushed Mediterranean sky. I'd never flown before.

'Everyone is smiling and friendly ... My ambition realised,' I crowed in my first postcard home. How invincible I felt, with my two T-shirts, cotton skirt sewn from a Laura Ashley offcut, white sandals and contraceptive pills. We toted Army surplus backpacks and sleeping bags, but slept rough only once in five weeks, in a municipal wash house, shooed away at daybreak by women thrashing their laundry against the granite ridges. I'd saved £60 from a job as a barmaid. Sue, who had a proper job, had £100, which meant she could afford souvenirs.

We had no guidebook, just a map and a pocket dictionary. We knew about Gaudí, though, and sought out his extraordinary buildings, covered in grime. We headed to the dim *barrio chino* (red-light district) for a cheap meal that launched a lifelong love affair with Spanish cuisine. Pasta soup, lamb chops, tomato salad, blackish wine from the jug, sweet fizzy water, egg flan. It became our staple diet, served wordlessly in inns where the choice was minimal.

We hitched to Huesca and experienced our first fiesta – buckets of wine and peaches, dancing in the street and the fierce sexual directness of boys thirsty for anything from beyond the Pyrenees, who quizzed us about Jean-Paul Sartre and Led Zeppelin. I fell for an easygoing lad with a Vespa who drove me to his old home, a dank ruin in the heart of town, and his new home, a cramped flat on the outskirts, where his mother laid a crisp embroidered cloth in my honour. I spilled red wine on it, but she cleared it away still smiling.

I refused to accompany him to the bullfight, which I thought cruel and barbaric, but amazingly managed to find him later in the tipsy torrent that poured from the bullring, and we roared into the pine-clad hills. This was boring for Sue, so we moved on, stopping short of our destination if a likely hill-top village came into view around lunch time. We avoided travelling in the afternoons, when drivers became drowsy or amorous.

We were both objects of curiosity with our fair skin, vast hair and sloppy gear, so we learned to deflect unwelcome approaches by being brisk. Spaniards, we concluded, were too dignified to foist themselves upon curt English women. Predators melted away or became allies after a crisp word and a chummy smile.

Lorries ruled the interminable single-lane highways, and hours rolled by while I tried to converse with drivers, sometimes – bravely, I thought – asking what they thought of Franco. One, in the intimacy of his cab, ventured a joke at the Caudillo's expense, about a toad, which escaped me, but I felt honoured by the confidence.

Two brothers took us in a smart car to their home in Madrid, whirled us round the capital by night, then installed us chastely in their absent parents' brocaded matrimonial bed. Next morning Sue and I found a hostel in a steep lane whose name, Cervantes, sounded promising, so we stayed a few days, bought greengages, honey, olives, sardines, lemons and brandy from shops nearby and trotted down the hill to the Prado to gaze at a single Velazquez, or a Goya.

We dined on pickled anchovies, spicy potatoes, fried squid, and shrimps whose husks we cast to the floor, then rolled home through the gloom and clapped our hands. The sound rang in the shuttered silence, summoning the night watchman who carried keys to every house in the street. With deep suspicion, he let us in.

Two philosophy students took us to Salamanca, where we sat in Spain's most beautiful square while the dark one composed, then recited, a poem, and the fair one bent his attention to Sue. But we hadn't come here to be entertained by intellectuals. Heading south, we smoked and drank with a couple of crop-haired conscripts until a pre-dawn hour, when they hurried for a train to their barracks. Lodgings became rougher. Once I turned on a tap and received an electric shock.

Two gypsies promised to take us to Granada, then explained that they were heading for Montilla to play guitar at a wine-tasting flamenco festival. They said they'd fix us up, say we were cousins. For the first time I felt uneasy, and on arrival asked the man in charge to help. 'I mean, it's obvious we're not their cousins, isn't it?' He gave us a room and a ticket for the event, worth a staggering five pounds each, a bottle of Montilla and a scarlet carnation. Beneath the Andalusian moon we sat up all night to a savagely thrilling flamenco; Franco belonged to a different time, and a different planet.

In 1972, the cheap way to Spain was on Laker Airways; Sir Freddie Laker had applied to fly 'no frills' between London and New York, but would have to wait another five years to be granted permission.

NEXT STOP, ULAN BATOR, 1972

To an eighteen-year-old looking for action, the Outer Hebrides might as well be Outer Mongolia, recalls Frank Partridge.

Some of my school chums went grape-picking in France. At least two teamed up with a bunch of hippies who were driving a bus to India – in those far-off days, it was relatively safe to take the direct route through Iraq and Afghanistan, although I never heard what happened to the magical mystery tourists. Someone else did a stint as a voluntary aid worker in Nepal. Me? I spent my gap year in Outer Mongolia. Well, I didn't actually, but it felt like it.

Shortly before the end of my schooldays, my parents decided to abandon urban living and move to the remotest spot in the British Isles: the Outer Hebrides. During that interminable summer, I received a letter from a waggish friend on what I now called 'the mainland', who wrote out my long and complicated new address, and after the line 'Outer Hebrides' helpfully added: 'Might as well be in Outer Mongolia.' I take it the sorting office was not amused. The letter took nine days to arrive from the south, via Newcastle upon Tyne.

For Ulan Bator, read Tarbert – the only significant settlement in the rocky, sandy, southern section of the Hebrides' largest island, which is called neither Lewis nor Harris, but both. Tarbert came into being because its harbour is protected from the full force of the sea by a long, narrow loch. A safe port in a storm for the fishing fleet, but a tricky proposition for the captain of the car ferry from Skye, which called twice a day. Getting in was straightforward, but getting out involved swinging the ship through a 180-degree turn on the nautical equivalent of a sixpence: a manoeuvre that attracted the nearest thing in Tarbert to a crowd.

Few other things did. Certainly not the Harris football team, who played in the summer because the incessant gales and darkness during the traditional soccer season precluded any form of outdoor activity. Even in May and June, the wind played havoc with my limited technique, and my team-mates were little better. That summer we trailed around the big island from one bleak outpost to another, losing every game. I failed to score in any of them, and was dropped.

Keeping in touch with the outside world was just as difficult. Radio reception was variable and a thick layer of interference obscured all but one of the TV channels. There was no nightlife to speak of, and no discernible life at all on the sacrosanct Sabbath (when hanging out the washing or taking a picnic was said to be frowned upon). There was no love interest; indeed, not much like-minded company of any sort. How could there be? Times may be changing now, but thirty years ago people who sold up in the south to build a new life in the Hebrides were branded 'White Settlers' – and largely left to their own devices and questionable, picnicking ways. So there was ample time to discover oneself and explore the wilderness: who needed Nepal?

In the north of Harris, I discovered the deserted moon-scape of mountain and peat bog, improbably traversed by a single-track road with passing places. It was here, while learning to drive, that I crashed a car for the first time, failing to avoid a sheep that chose the precise moment of my arrival to forgo its day-long grazing and career into the road. My mum's Mini was severely dented, but the sheep, after a moment's rumination, dusted itself down and shot off across the moor, apparently unscathed.

While the north had a certain wild grandeur, it was the 25 miles south from Tarbert to Rodel where Harris really came into its own. On the eastern coast, the oldest rocks in the world had been stripped of their soil, the coastline pummelled into submission by the sea. The road twists in and out, through, round, under and over coves and cliffs, inlets and promontories, and a hundred pools and lochs. Nature at her most uncompromising. Before the road was built in the 1930s, the dead had to be carried in their coffins across the moors to the west, because there was insufficient soil in the east to bury them. Cairns mark the places where the pallbearers paused for a rest – and, no doubt, a stiffening drop of something to help them on their way.

The western coast could not be more different. The land sweeps gently down to the Atlantic breakers, separated from them by Caribbean-like strips of brilliant white sand – deserted, of course, apart from the birds and the seals. Clear summer evenings seemed to last forever, as the sun's shallow, downward curve barely dipped below the horizon before reappearing, renewed, to start the new day. In the giant, russet sky, there was often a glimmering suspicion of the Northern Lights. My father took great delight in demonstrating to visitors that it was possible to read a newspaper in the garden at midnight. Nature at her most benign.

But for an eighteen-year-old impatient to unlock the secrets of the world, the timing was all wrong. One day, I boarded a fishing boat and sailed to the offshore island of Pabbay, populated only by rabbits and a herd of a few hundred deer. I climbed to the top of the central hill and watched as hunters moved in for the annual cull. Their long and patient stalking ended with a dozen resounding shots. Job done. Silence returned. The sea rolled in from all sides. A distant figure signalled that it was time to leave. I hurried down a boggy slope towards the jetty, slipped and fell awkwardly, and heard the crack of my ankle a fraction of a second before I passed out.

When I came to, I lay on my back in the damp bracken, unable to walk, staring at the sky as the gulls and corncrakes screeched and wheeled. I had no sense of time, and was sure the boat had left without me. I was young and carefree in a part of the world that I realise now is as close to paradise as you can find, but on that day in that summer – that lonely summer of 1972 – it seemed the worst possible place to be.

The summer hit in 1972 was 'American Pie' by Don McLean.

A RELENTLESSLY AND UPROARIOUSLY CONVIVIAL WELCOME, 1973

'I was eighteen years old, very easily impressed and took myself extremely seriously.' During a German summer Linda Cookson learned seven new words for drunkenness.

August 1973. Gary Glitter was 'Leader of the Gang' at the top of the British charts. The Watergate scandal was breaking. And I and my boyfriend of the time were spending the whole of that summer in Germany together, equipped with a Collins Mini Gem Deutsch–English dictionary and a supply of tinned corned beef (in case we didn't like the food). We were doing a holiday job before going to college in October and it was the first time I had ever been out of the country. I was eighteen years old, very easily impressed and took myself extremely seriously. The perfect profile for the innocent abroad.

We were working as translators for a wine company in the Rhineland. The bottling plant and company offices were in Burg Layen, a small village nestling snugly amid the ranks of vine terraces built back from the river Nahe. The area was filled with timbered, white-walled houses bearing paintings of bunches of grapes and beaming countrywomen (which I considered hugely tasteful at the time). And the air was sweet with alcohol. During that summer in Germany I learned seven new words for varieties of drunkenness. Sadly for my liver, it marked the beginning of the end of my hitherto puritanical aversion to wine-drinking.

Our job included translating promotional material. I learned all about the differences between Spatlese and

Auslese, and between Beerenauslese and Trockenbeerenaus-lese – right through to defining the tooth-rotting sweetness of Eiswein. I learned to write things like 'with an elegant bouquet' without laughing. But, above all, I got to grips with the important business of wine-sampling.

The neighbourhood was relentlessly and uproariously convivial. From village to village there were wine festivals every weekend. There were festivals to say an emotional farewell to the last vintage and to empty the barrels in readiness for the next. There were festivals to try out the new vintage, and compare it enthusiastically with those of previous years. And then there were the local 'Kirmes' festivals – a particularly riotous set of celebrations, held in honour of each village's special saint. It was, if only in theory, a strongly Catholic area.

I soon learned that Rhineland wine villages looked sleepy by day only, because they were snoozing off their hangovers. Come nightfall, it would always be party time again. Whole villages were transformed into gypsy camps, blazing with fairy lights and crammed with sideshows, food stalls and a forest of beer and wine tents. Early on in the summer, at one of those food stalls, I had a further fatal taste of corruption – a paper tray of *Currywurst* (German sausage smothered in raw curry powder and a dollop of ketchup), which I embraced as the height of sophistication and attempted to reproduce subsequently at many a dinner party back home.

The corned beef never got eaten. We were too overwhel-med by hospitality, as people bombarded us with invitations to suppers of sauerbraten (a delicious regional pot roast) and streuselkuchen (a sort of cherry crumble cake). It was as a guest at one of those suppers that I ate my very first frozen pizza. It took a few more years before the UK caught on to that particular treat.

We were a local curiosity. Everybody in the village seemed to know about us – something I put down to personal charisma at the time. In truth, I now realise, we were unmissable: my boyfriend with his lion's mane of red hair and penchant for purple loons, myself in full and flowing pre-Raphaelite regalia topped and tailed with a cowboy hat and a pair of desert boots. At this point, the miniskirt – by then definitely *démodé* back in England – had only just hit the Rhineland.

When I think back to that summer I remember it with huge affection. I remember the evening of our very first day at work, when the company boss took us to a Carole King concert in Frankfurt and we all held up lighted matches and sang 'You Got a Friend'. I remember betting on a horse at Baden-Baden on the assumption that age was a sign of experience, and being dumbfounded when my nag hobbled home last. I remember countless excursions, courtesy of workmates and their families, to mountains and castles and riverside beauty spots.

It was a great time. I arrived back in England in early October with a wine enthusiasm, a *Currywurst* addiction and a cigarette habit (born – I'm ashamed to say – of the discovery that you could put British 5p coins into the 1DM slot of German cigarette machines). I also had an embarrassingly large stash of Deutschmarks. We had been ludicrously well paid by English standards and no one had allowed us to spend any money. I bought the latest Leonard Cohen album, a copy of *The Little Prince* and a new pair of desert boots, and got ready for the business of being a student.

As a response to the Arab oil crisis, British motorists began to be issued with fuel ration books on 29 November 1973.

In the event, rationing was not implemented; instead, a nationwide 50mph limit was imposed. By the time of the next election in February 1974, the price of petrol had risen to 50p per gallon (9p per litre).

GETTING STONED WAS A BAD EXPERIENCE, 1973

Back in 1973, Angus Frazer and the Shah were alive and unpopular and in Iran.

I had never been stoned before, at least not in the biblical sense. I wasn't sure how to handle it. I plodded on until one of my assailants scored a direct hit on my left temple, whereupon my self-control and I parted company. I bent down, grabbed a handy piece of Marand mountain roadside and hurled it at my persecutors. It was sheer luck that one of them intercepted my lack of aim; there was a loud cry and to my amazement they disappeared.

The backpacking fraternity hadn't introduced themselves to the Persians in 1973. They just spluttered through on aged buses to Afghanistan where the hash was cheap. If I had any doubts that I was a pioneer, those Kurdish youths dispelled them.

Next day I arrived in Tehran, and returned to the 12th century. I approached an imposing bank in the city centre, to change some money. The commissionaire looked doubtfully at my threadbare shorts, but let me pass. As the doors whispered shut behind me, the horn-blaring, heat-blistered inferno of Tehran was replaced by a delicious, cool silence. The marble hall swept before me to the foot of a grand staircase, totally empty. I knew how Alice in Wonderland would have felt at the bottom of the rabbit hole.

I paused, then tried the first door on the right. A boardroom table was surrounded by a group that looked as if they could be the governors of the Iranian Central Bank. I hurriedly tried to withdraw, but before I could free my rucksack from the doorjamb, one of the Savile Row suits arose and inquired in impeccable English if he could help me. The Persian banking system halted while I was ushered politely through the corridors of power to the public halls where I could change my ten pounds into rials.

A week later hospitality joined courtesy on the roll of Persian virtues. I was in a remote village on the shores of the Caspian Sea, sipping a rose-petal sherbet and studying my map, when a minor problem presented itself. The road back to civilisation carried about six motorised vehicles a day. Off the beaten track in Persia nobody really understood what a hitchhiker was, and I could envisage spending weeks travelling to Isfahan, my next destination.

Luckily, though, all Persians travelled by bus, and the smallest outposts boasted remarkably good services. So I headed for the bus station. The man in the ticket office and I got on famously. Despite my elementary grasp of Persian he perceived that I wished to catch a bus and mimed in return that it departed at six and a half.

I reported at six, just as my friend was shutting up for the night. A flaw in our communication became apparent. The bus left at six-thirty the next morning. This was serious news. I was a good sleeper, and my chances of waking up at 5.30 a.m. on a Caspian beach without an alarm clock were zero. Umar smiled. There was no problem. I was to have dinner and sleep at his house. Then he could ensure that I caught the bus.

The house was a large building, ranged around a central courtyard. Each wall had a veranda: the effect was like a miniature cloister. We sat on the floor around a beautiful Persian carpet on which were placed dishes of lamb, rice yoghurt and sauces. I was squatting on my haunches, when an animated discussion developed, apparently about my clothes. Umar beckoned me through to his bedroom, produced a splendid pair of the baggy trousers, and motioned me to put them on. I was bemused by this ritual, but returned to the dining room dressed in Umar's best. As I again squatted down to eat, the room dissolved in laughter. The family realised that I actually preferred squatting to sitting, and had not been protecting my filthy jeans from their spotless floor.

Iran was a jigsaw of fascination, and I was sad when it was time to begin my long hitchhike home. Just outside Tehran I was picked up by a juggernaut. It was raining by the time we reached Tabriz and up in the mountains the temperature had plummeted. Beyond the town the road continued to climb, winding up each successive ridge and snaking down each valley. On a clear day we might have seen Ararat to the north. Now, however, night had fallen, and the headlights fought to slice through the wall of the rain.

The driver was singing in a nasal falsetto interrupted by frequent yawns. He gesticulated emphatically – would I take over the driving? But I had no desire to start learning how to control a heavy goods vehicle with two fully laden trailer units, on potholed hairpins, in a thunderstorm at night – and in a foreign country. Instead, I just shouted at him every few seconds to keep him awake.

The following year a guide to Iran was published, including tips on backpacking. I suppose it would have been useful; but then usefulness must be weighed against the delights of the unexpected.

For those with less ambitious itineraries, the favoured way to leave Britain in the summer of 1973 was with a rail ticket to 'Toutes Gares Belge' – any station in Belgium –

issued by the Transalpino student travel company. It cost £6 from London, and allowed travel as far as the Luxembourg or German border. Soon afterwards, Transalpino went bust. The 'Toutes Gares Belge' concept was reintroduced by Eurostar in 2003.

ON A ROAD TO NOWHERE, 1973

Thirty years ago, Simon Calder went hitching around Ireland. In summer 2003 he returned to see if it's still as difficult to reach the next village.

Seven days may be a long time in politics; but seven hours beside the empty Dungarvan coast road is an age. To give you some idea how dismal the hitchhiking was in the summer of '73, the driver who eventually gave me a lift had passed me, travelling in the opposite direction, at 9.30 a.m., just two hours into my wait. He had time to drive into Cork, present a three-hour radio show, enjoy a relaxed lunch and head back. On his way to work he had made a mental note, he told me during the brief time we spent together, to pick me up on his way home. He knew that on a Sunday morning in a desolate stretch of County Cork, nothing much was going anywhere.

That long, cool and mostly damp summer, even when I did get a ride it was often so short that it barely registered. Most Irish drivers are, and were, generous to a fault. But the horizons of many motorists in the Republic seem to extend no further than the end of the village. Hitchhikers accustomed to measuring lifts in hundreds of miles, not hundreds of yards, are forced to recalibrate expectations. It took an implausible 24 lifts to travel from Kinsale in County Cork to the port of Rosslare on the Wexford coast, a distance of 145 miles.

Today, that's 233 kilometres, or at least it is on some of the destination boards by the roadside. Anyone who frets that the special character of Ireland has been devoured by the

Celtic Tiger economy or subsumed by Europeanisation need only address the puzzle facing every visitor to Ireland: as distances are measured officially in kilometres, why does any half-decent cluster of road signs sport at least a handful of leftovers that still mark miles, and why are the speed limits, even on new signs, measured in miles per hour? (The official tourist road map offers help with road signs. It shows a red circle with '30' in the middle. The legend explains: 'Speed limit of 48kph.')

Thirty summers ago, the further-flung corners of the Republic were still defying the arrival two years earlier of decimal currency. And the question that travelled with me on a fortnight that involved more hiking than hitching was: how can a land so welcoming and beautiful be so empty?

South-west Ireland was Europe's backwater, a beguiling wilderness for someone brought up amid the artless bricks and mortar of an English New Town. On a screen as wide as the sky, dramatic weather fronts rolled in much more frequently than passing cars. The sun, when permitted, would daub the hillsides with Impressionist tones, before surrendering to another wave of rain clouds.

The tent that served as my shelter never quite dried out in an itinerary that took me from the ferry at Rosslare up to Dublin, across to Killarney, around the Ring of Kerry and skirting the shoreline to Kinsale. I had heard that this was where hippies congregated, the closest the British Isles got to Kathmandu. This handsome, historic port wasn't Nirvana. But it was better than working on a dairy farm at the end of Gatwick airport's runway, with a herd of traumatised cows, for £11 a week. So long as you hitchhiked, that could get you to Ireland for a couple of weeks. The main expense was the £3 overnight ferry fare from Fishguard to Rosslare (it has now risen to £23). The battered old Sealink vessel fought an unholy battle with a summer storm that subsided only as the ferry arrived along with the dawn.

The police were waiting for me. Indeed, the gardai at Rosslare port were waiting to check every passenger leaving the ferry, since terrorism was escalating. But I managed to race out of the terminal in time to catch the cars as they drove ashore, and dozed all the way to Dublin in one of them. Back then, the Irish capital had the air of a provincial British city in an advanced stage of decay, rather than the confident, vibrant metropolis it is today. But at least you could get free Guinness at the St James's Gate Brewery after an hour's tour. (Today, it has been turned into a tourist trap, the Storehouse – admission £10.)

A long day's hitch across a misty landscape ended with a night sleeping in a farmer's car. I arrived in Killorglin just as the Puck Fair was beginning. As I nursed a single pint through a long, light evening, I asked when the pubs closed. 'October.'

In 2003, to reach the west of Ireland takes about an hour and, if you time your booking and flight right, costs £20. No-frills airlines have deprived a generation of the experience of sleeping fitfully by the roadside; good for them. But hitching is still feasible, and the magical countryside is undiminished. On the N22 between Killarney and that tricky turn-off for Kinsale, low, brooding mountains crowd in on a road that dips and swerves southeastwards.

As a teenager with long hair and a Belgian army greatcoat, I was often capable of waiting for seven hours, even with loads of traffic going past. Thirty years on, hitching has become easier, though an improbable number of Irish drivers still make a circular motion with their forefinger that signifies, 'I'm driving to the end of the village then turning around and heading straight back.' And, invariably, they do.

When a car stops, it is likely to be faster, more comfortable, and going further. In a straggle of houses that goes by the name of Crookstown, Jackie O'Callaghan stopped for me. She was driving for a full 20 miles (or should that be 32km?), a veritable odyssey in Irish hitchhiking. Inconveniently, our prospective paths diverged half a mile down the road. Being a generous and hospitable soul, she felt obliged to divert to Kinsale, a good 15 miles away from Cork, her final destination, while regaling me with tales of rural life in 21st-century Ireland.

Jackie dropped me outside the Tap Tavern. I am sure I recognised Mary, the landlady, after all these years. But I didn't summon up the nerve to ask how, in 1973, three pints of Murphy's could total exactly 50p. The fortunes of Kinsale have risen along with the price of stout. Freshly painted primary colours on smart restaurants and bumper-to-bumper BMWs signify that this fishing port has become a middle-class holiday haven.

The signpost pointing the way home has not changed in thirty years. In 1973, it took me three days to hitch back to Crawley from this point. In 2003, a few minutes after I left the Tap Tavern, a car stopped. Like the lift I took from the same spot thirty years earlier, it was going only as far as Cork airport. Then, as now, I jumped out and thanked the driver. But this time I hopped on a plane that took me to London for only slightly more than the weekly agricultural wage in the summer of '73.

On 1 January 1973 the UK joined the European Economic Community.

A SMALL, PUNGENT AND CURIOUSLY EXOTIC CONTINENT, 1974

When Jonathan Glancey worked his way across the floor of a London factory, it was like a trip around the world.

Student summers were wonderful. Here, at last, away from the languors of ivory towers, was a chance to work. Knuckle down, get your hands dirty, earn your keep, pay off bills and save for a holiday. And often the job was as much of an adventure as the subsequent travels.

Of all the workshops in all the world, I felt most at home at Bristol-Myer, South Ruislip. This was a scion of a US cosmetics corporation that had taken root off London's arterial Western Avenue in a low-lying Art-Deco inspired factory. Bristol-Myer made Mum Rolette, Clairol hair conditioner, Ingram shaving cream and a canned drink called Nutrament, a zillion-caloried pick-me-up for athletes that tasted, deliciously, of fruit-flavoured and only slightly diluted condensed milk.

A suburban factory making nothing I would want in adult life might seem an odd favourite. But what I learned in that pungent factory was a simple truth. You can travel to the most exotic places on earth, seek out the greatest adventures, but feel as much an outsider as the narrator in Camus' *L'Etranger*. The crowd at Bristol-Myer, save for one grisly old foreman, were a family of sorts writ large and Radio One loud. Broken up into clearly defined and jealous empires – Production, Warehouse, Goods-In, Goods-Out and Export – this industrial family met together in the bright mezzanine canteen or else sprawled across the manicured factory lawn during dinner break.

The student's privilege was to work across departments, now making wooden cases in which to pack delicate goods, now whizzing around the warehouse on a red electric fork-lift truck, cleaning production-line machinery, loading and unloading lorries, sweeping yards and chatting to everyone.

Crossing departments was, nevertheless, a bit like travelling from country to country, each with its own government, customs and laws. Chubby, easy-come, easy-go Brian, with the Elvis quiff, ran Goods-In with Peter, an ex-serviceman who spun tea-break tales of the whores and bordellos of the world. Richard, with the Hendrix-inspired 'Afro' hair, ruled Export. Richard was slight and highly strung and dreamed of doing something 'better'. He worked like a Trojan, but in between rowed furiously with Karol, an ex-Polish Squadron fighter pilot, once based at nearby Northolt, who had stalwartly refused to improve his English since he arrived here in 1939. Karol was in his late sixties, could lift hundredweight barrels of hair oil as if they were individual cans of Nutrament, drove an ancient two-tone Hillman Minx and called everyone who crossed him a 'putana'. Mick, the handsome, middle-aged Irishman laughed the day away alongside them, winking and 'Jesusing' wryly, as Karol and Richard 'effed' and 'putanaed' to the accompaniment of saws, drills, hammers and nails.

A second Mick dominated the warehouse. A gossip without equal, he pirouetted across the lino floors in his nifty fork-lift truck, exchanging news and cutting asides, cackling with laughter and employing the Saxon word for 'I thrust' as only lucid Celts know how.

Mick, who I liked because he despised General Franco (who still had a year before Hell claimed him), enjoyed verbal fisticuffs with Reg, deputy-foreman from Production and last

of the old-time, shirt-and-tie gentleman workers. Reg introduced me to *The Ragged Trousered Philanthropists*, 'Cassandra'
and any number of ranting, digging, shaking and otherwise
dissenting texts. He was critical of the Soviet Union and had
much to say about my holiday designed to take me to Japan
via the Trans-Siberian Railway.

The land of Goods-Out was overseen by two of the most
perfect industrial knights I have ever met. Bert (who drove
an immaculate Morris 1100 as if it were a classic Bentley) and
John (who wobbled along on a Honda 50) sported spotless
white coats and, if they were ever ruffled on a long, hot
summer afternoon, never showed it. John talked obsessively
of black silk stockings and suspenders as he took stock of
hair spray and shaving cream, leaning back in his battered
black-plastic swivel chair, whilst Bert, quiet and dignified,
kept underarm deodorants rolling effortlessly across the
armpits of Europe.

Bristol-Myer women were confined to the purdah of
Production, or else ran the canteen. There was the gorgeous
Ingrid who wore short skirts and black stockings, drove John
of Despatch delirious, but wanted me to date her. There was
the wonderful lady with silver hair and manners that made
the Queen Mum's look a bit gor-blimey, who ran the canteen
and told everyone how lovely they looked. There was Linda
with the staggeringly dirty jokes and even dirtier laugh and
a gaggle of the youngest white girls who spent tea and dinner
breaks relating the night before's disco-action. 'And she goes,
and I go, and, tee hee, this bloke this and my mum says . . .'
I could never get enough of it.

By the end of eight weeks, I felt fit (lifting, shoving,
tugging and pulling on a Popeye-strong diet of Nutrament)
and comfortably off (my £18.50 a week basic was doubled
most weeks with overtime and Saturday mornings). Most of

all I felt I belonged. Since 1974, I have travelled extensively and have had many adventures, but Bristol-Myer remains in my mind as a small, pungent and curiously exotic continent all of its own.

On 1 October 1974, Britain's first branch of McDonald's opened in Woolwich, southeast London.

AGHIOS IOANNIS – THE MISSING YEARS, 1974

In Corfu, David Orkin fell in love with the hostel, the village, the taverna . . . and the table football game.

In 1974, at the age of sixteen, I bought a ticket for a two-week charter flight to Corfu and wrote to both of the island's youth hostels asking about availability for my chosen dates. Though I've yet to receive a reply from the Kondokali hostel, I did receive a friendly, positive letter from Vasili Combolitis, the manager at Aghios Ioannis. The hostel was housed in a three-storey villa built by the British in the 1860s and surrounded by fields, gardens and olive groves. At the top of a hill in the centre of the island, both the building and the adjacent palm tree were visible for miles. The beaches were well over an hour's walk away.

I immediately fell in love with the place: the hostel, the village, Costa's taverna where we ate every evening, the beaches (especially Pelekas and the unspoilt Myrtiotissa), the sunny days and balmy evenings, the life. So much so that I found myself going back year after year. Sometimes I camped in the garden. You could also pitch a tent below the village in Costa's fields (known as Strawberry Fields and Cactus Hilton). There was no charge, the understanding being that you would eat your meals at his taverna.

Costa's taverna was the centre of village life, especially in the evenings: the food was excellent and cheap, and he, wife Nitsa and daughters Lula and Anna were loved by everyone who passed through. There was a jukebox which, in addition to a few Greek dancing favourites, had the cream of late 60s and early 70s rock, including classics by Neil Young, Hendrix and the Doors. Outside wobbled a heavily used table-football game – in later years we'd buy souvlakias from Nikos the Kebab Man just so that we could use the greasy paper they were wrapped in to oil the table's metal rods and keep the wooden players spinning freely.

Brits, Germans and Swedes flocked to Aghios Ioannis. Long-haul air travel was fearsomely expensive in those days, and Greece was a much-used hub on overland and sea routes. Corfu was offered as a free stopover on all the ferries between Italy and Greece. Many travellers came to the island intending just to break their journey for a night or two and ended up staying at Aghios Ioannis for the summer – and returning the following year.

In the evening, in the village, people would sit at the taverna's long tables and swap stories of their recent experiences in Goa, Malindi, Phuket, Bali, Kathmandu or Cuzco over dinner. They'd pause occasionally to feed a few drachs into the jukebox, or to wander off for a discreet smoke. Local Greek guys would strut their funky stuff, dancing with a glass on their head or perhaps a table or chair clenched between their teeth. When they'd stopped eating the furniture, they would promise undying love to any passing female traveller.

Eventually, in the small hours, Costa would turn off the jukebox and close the taverna. We'd adjourn to the hostel garden. Someone would produce a guitar and massacre the latest hit by Cat Stevens, James Taylor or Dylan. Finally, a road down to Pelakis beach was started. The game was up.

On my last visit (in 1981) I turned up to find that the hostel had closed. I didn't have a tent with me, much to the delight of the mosquitoes and sandflies. The Corfu bubble had finally burst. For a few years afterwards I'd hear bits of

Corfu news through the grapevine – the table-football game had fallen to bits, the jukebox had gone, the hostel had reopened as a hotel – but it eventually faded.

More than twenty years on, I decided to go back. I disembarked from the ferry to Corfu Town's harbour side. After two decades would there be any remnants of how things had been? I found the bus stop with ease but was surprised to see that its sign said 'Aghios Ioannis – For Aqualand Water Fun Park'. Though Corfu is a lush and verdant isle, the village had long been known for its chronic water shortages: coming back from the beach and going for a shower only to find the water off was a daily irritation.

On the bus ride I saw that the builders had not been idle. We passed Aqualand, an incongruous, multicoloured monstrosity that looked strangely like the Pompidou Centre. It had been built on the site of a marshy pond in a field about a mile from the village.

At the Aghios Ioannis bus terminus things were familiar: Dino's Taverna (our alternative to Costa's in the evening) had become 'Dino's Supermarket' and looked to have closed down relatively recently. More new buildings on the ten-minute walk to the village proper: I paused before rounding the last corner.

Amazingly it didn't look that different. The 'hostel' was now the Hotel Marinda, freshly painted and with flags fluttering outside. The taverna had new white plastic tables and chairs, and there were a few more cars around. And there was Costa wiping down a table. He saw me as I drew nearer, shouted to the kitchen and his wife and two daughters appeared. Costa was now well into his seventies. I asked about accommodation. Anna, his daughter, offered me a nice, simple room in her pension just behind the taverna, for £10 a night.

Over the next few days she helped fill in the missing Corfu years. The discovery of underground water had put an end to the shortages, and helped to create Aqualand. The final nail was hammered into the coffin of the 'old' Aghios Ioannis nine years ago when Costa stopped allowing camping in his fields.

Anna's sister Lula had brought her English husband back to live in the village. The two women, and Anna's husband, help in the taverna. Costa still works from early morning until midnight every day.

The taverna's inside walls are covered with hundreds of photos of past revellers. A Dutch holiday company had 'discovered' Aghios Ioannis and block-books the rooms in the hotel (now managed once again by Vasili, and named after his daughter). Pelekas beach has a big hotel and lots of apartment buildings: there still isn't a sealed road down to Myrtiotissa but a lot of cars and motorbikes bump down the dusty steep dirt road to the beach, where you can now hire sun beds and umbrellas.

Virtually unknown when I'd last been there, Myrtiotissa was already busy in the middle of June. Anna said that quite a few 'old-timers' still come back to visit, often bringing their partners and children to show them the mythical place associated with so many happy, faded memories. Before the jukebox had been taken away, a bunch of Irish regulars had taped all the records on it and left the tapes at the taverna for posterity.

On the last evening of my pilgrimage, I sat with my back to the taverna building, persuaded Costa to play one of those tapes and looked around. The taverna's tables were occupied by quiet Dutch families with young children. The cicadas still buzzed and the evening air was full of remembered scents of jasmine and wild herbs.

It was great to come back, wonderful to see Costa, Nitsa, Lula and Anna again, to know that Myrtiotissa hadn't yet been completely ruined and that village life still meant tranquil mornings and lazy afternoons. Though I should have known better I couldn't help hankering after the crazy days I remember so well. Aghios Ioannis had grown up and mellowed, but I suppose I haven't.

On 13 March 1974, Charles de Gaulle airport opened in Paris.

ALL'S FAIR IN LOVE AND WAR, 1974

Back in 1974 Monica Troughton set off for Mykonos on a heavenly pursuit.

I pushed him out of the way too late. Not only had Richard knocked the contact lens off my finger; he'd squashed it with his foot. I'd removed the lens to clean it. At that moment Richard had stood back to read the departure notices. We'd collided. 'I'm so sorry. I had no idea you were just . . .' Our flight was called.

It was 1974 and we were on our way to Greece. Christopher had arranged this holiday, although the three of us didn't know each other very well. Christopher the Greek god. Christopher's every movement reflected the stirring of his soul. His stature was proud. His features were radiant. I wanted to poke Richard's eyes out. We were competing for Christopher's attention. The way Richard swooned all over him left no doubt as to his sexual orientation.

We boarded the plane. We both wanted to sit next to Christopher. Christopher sat in the middle. We drank champagne. The wings of the plane shimmered against the setting sun.

Athens airport was hot. I fell down three steps of the escalator. I resembled a braying donkey, hoofs clawing at baked earth as I tried to gauge the whereabouts of the step with my one good eye. Christopher was too busy being flattered by Richard to notice.

We scoured Athens for a hotel. Eventually we were offered a twin-bedded room. We took it. We went downstairs to eat. Five men, wild and ugly, were drinking at the bar. One of the men jumped up and grabbed the owner by the collar. I told Richard to do something. He said he needed a tablet, and reached for the ridiculous little leather underarm bag he carried. The owner ushered us to a table. Water and ouzo were put before us. One of the men sauntered over and put his hands on Richard's shoulders. Richard froze. Christopher boldly introduced us all.

The man wore a T-shirt with a dagger dipped in blood on the front. His nose was short and broad. Richard sat like a caged animal. 'The Kray Twins? You know the Kray Twins?' the man asked. Silence. Christopher coughed, 'Yes, I knew their mother!' The T-shirt man cheered. The owner passed him bottles of everything. We ate bread, dolmades and koftas, and drank. We toasted Mrs Kray at least a dozen times an hour.

I do not recollect going to bed. I opened an eye. The other was swollen and stuck. It still had a contact lens in it. Cars were hooting, people were shouting, flies were everywhere. I leaped to the mirror. I squeezed out the lens, popped it in a glass and glanced at the bed. It was Richard's solitary head I saw. 'Richard, where's Christopher?' Richard hung his head low over the edge of the bed and was sick into his deck shoes. I grabbed a towel and a glass. I poured him water. He drank and crunched. Crunched? He'd eaten my contact lens. I began to howl.

The door burst open. Christopher, looking as though he'd spent the night at a health farm, declared the T-shirt man to be the best lover he'd ever had. He was now ready to travel. We eventually left the hotel: Richard and I in silence, Christopher singing the whole way to the ferry. .

I'd never heard of Mykonos, but at first sight I loved every inch of it. Our room had a balcony overlooking the sea. It all looked heavenly, but I was soon confined to three days indoors – my front was strawberry red and swollen.

On the fifth day Christopher and Richard suggested we go to a beach. I could lie in the shade. After a while, though, I'd had enough of the running commentary on the white sands, the beach café and the nude males, and set off for a stroll. I trod carefully. I was aware of scorpions and snakes. I sneaked on an old pair of glasses I'd found in my basket; they had one arm missing and one lens was cracked, but they would do. In the sharp white rocks I spotted a chameleon; it was both fascinating and terrifying. I bent down to observe it and my glasses fell off. I heard a strange noise from behind a rock. I peered round it. There I saw three naked men, lying on their backs. I backed away and fell into the snake-infested grass, where I screamed hysterically. The men swooped around me. I flapped like a penguin. They helped me up. My glasses were in that grass. I decided to leave them. I wasn't sure whether I wanted to see any more. I just wanted to go back to my room. I had no idea what I was going to write on my postcards.

I needn't have worried. There was to be no more postal service, no phones, no ferries. War had been declared between Greece and Turkey. All Greek males were to be taken off the island at dawn. Christopher and Richard looked dismayed. Mrs Andronikos, the landlady, needed comforting. I followed her into her apartment. A table, bed and kitchen all in one huge room. Mrs Andronikos fed me. She brought me crumpled black-and-white photographs. She gave me a pair of her late husband's glasses. We drank retsina. We laughed. The sun set across the bay. Red rays poured into the room illuminating Mrs Andronikos's beautiful Greek face. She gave me coffee, strong and black. She was 77. I was 23.

At 6 a.m., as arranged, I tapped on her door. She was ready for a week's leave – her daughter was taking over. Mrs Andronikos took me to a friend: a farmer who showed us round the island in his cart. We sauntered past chapels, hills and beaches. We trotted through little lanes. We ate tomatoes and goats' cheeses; I felt healthy, confident and alive. For me, the war was nowhere to be seen.

Returning, I ran straight to our room. I was looking forward to seeing Christopher and Richard. But as I pushed the door open I saw Richard lying on the bed, an empty bottle of pills by his side. He was still breathing. I shouted around the house. Mrs Andronikos put on a shawl and raced to fetch the doctor.

I waited outside the room as the doctor brought Richard round. I heard groaning, retching, slapping noises. Mrs Andronikos offered me another room, but I wanted to be near Richard. I left a note on the door for Christopher but he never returned. Richard wept. He'd given Christopher everything – his body, soul and cigarette lighter. After that, he spent each day on the balcony sipping soup. The war was almost over, and soon the ship would take us back.

Mrs Andronikos and I shared a last evening together. We ate, hugged, drank and laughed. Then we cried. She gave me a trinket and a tobacco pouch. I packed Christopher's things and gave them to her, in case he came back.

Mrs Andronikos and I promised to pray for each other and to write. I promised to return, and blubbed all the way to Athens. I never heard from Christopher again. Richard and I arranged to meet, but when we did so he was cold and distant. The friendship was lost.

Mrs Andronikos and I wrote all through the winter. I agreed I would spend the summer with her. I was making arrangements when a letter arrived from Greece. Mrs Andronikos had died. Her daughter had written to inform me that the guesthouse was to be sold. No other holiday has compacted so many events as that one. Sometimes I stray back to the memory.

What had brought it to mind this time? My eighteen-year-old daughter had informed me that she and a friend were about to book a holiday together. What, if anything, did I know about Mykonos?

On 16 August 1974, the Court Line–Clarkson's–Horizon package holiday conglomerate went bust, stranding 40,000 holidaymakers abroad and leaving 100,000 more who had paid but had yet to travel with no compensation.

SOMETHING ABOUT THE ACCENT, 1975

Cathy Packe loses her lisp and learns to speak like a true Guadalajareña.

A thirteen-hour flight is a long one when you have never been on a plane before. By the age of nineteen I had travelled a bit in Europe, but only to those parts that could reasonably be reached by ferry and road. Mexico by land and sea would probably have been feasible during the long student vacation, when I planned to travel, but common sense told me to fly. So I booked the cheapest ticket I could find – this was in the days before Freddie Laker invented the Skytrain – and set off for Los Angeles, and a connecting flight down to Guadalajara, Mexico's second city.

At this point I was a year into a Spanish course at Durham University, and I was expected to spend some time before my second year learning a few linguistic subtleties from the natives. It would have been easier to go to Spain, of course, but thanks to a grant from a local foundation I had more money than I expected to help me get there. Since the whole trip was regarded as part of the course, the Spanish department had a veto over every student's plans, so backpacking around aimlessly wasn't really an option – although in retrospect it might have benefited my Spanish more than the course on which I enrolled myself.

Guadalajara University ran – and probably still does – a summer school for American students, who got credits towards their degrees simply by turning up. I took classes in Mexican history and culture, and although by the end I had a grasp of Aztec civilisation and the reasons for the Revolution, five weeks of lectures in English made little impression on my linguistic skills.

The opportunity to speak Spanish didn't arise until after classes were over for the day. I spent my time in Guadalajara staying with a delightful Mexican family, who had a large house in an elegant residential district close to the Country Club. They liked to take in students, even though they had six children of their own, most of whom were grown-up and still living at home. They were all happy to chat to their four summer students, particularly, or so I thought, to me. I soon realised that they were amused by my accent, copied until this point from teachers who had learned their own Spanish in Spain. Mexicans find the Castilian lisp indescribably funny, preferring a pronunciation that is far more sibilant. Immediately, I stopped caring about increasing my vocabulary and improving my grammar; all that mattered was that I should learn to sound like a Mexican – and, in particular, a Guadalajareña.

Mexico's second city is a splendid antidote to the manic capital. Guadalajara is a lively, attractive city founded by the Spanish in 1542, with a colonial-style main square, surrounded by arcades and shaded cafés. The four of us spent our free time exploring, and sometimes we went out of town, riding in the countryside, or visiting local beauty spots. One excursion took us to a town on the Pacific coast some 200 miles away, a journey of six hours on a long-distance bus that had seen many better days. Our destination was a small place with a long, unspoiled sandy beach and a few tiny hotels. Most of the roads seemed to be little more than dirt tracks, so we were happy to hitch a ride around with some of the local boys, who had hired an open-topped jeep. This village, Puerto Vallarta, is now one of Mexico's main Pacific coast resorts; back in the summer of '75, none of the main hotel chains had thought of moving in.

Despite their jokes at my expense, the Capetillo family and I became good friends. Towards the end of my stay they were part of a plan to celebrate my birthday, two of the sons persuading me to come with them to pick up some shopping, a pretext for driving me to a restaurant where a surprise party was to take place. We stayed in touch long after I had left Mexico. I still exchange news with one of them, nearly thirty years after we first met; and while I was living for a time in the United States, she invited me to her home in Chicago to spend Thanksgiving with her family.

After five weeks the course came to an end and, university requirements satisfied, I set off to explore some more of the country: the colonial town of Cuernavaca; Oaxaca with its colourful native Indian population; the ruins of Teotihuacan; and Mexico City, with its intoxicating mixture of ancient and modern, noise and crowds. Eventually I had to get back to Los Angeles for the flight home, a 24-hour journey by bus, which by now was all I could afford. The trip was interminable, punctuated every two or three hours by a stop, an opportunity to buy snacks and chat to fellow passengers. Most of them had never heard of England, imagining it to be somewhere near New York, the furthest outpost they could imagine.

The driver was entranced to have a foreigner on his bus, especially one who had never seen a desert, let alone driven across one. He made the other passengers move around so that I could sit at the front, near enough to hear his comments on the passing landscape. At one point we made an unscheduled stop on the roadside, where he made me get out of the bus. Below us was a sheer drop, at the bottom of which I could see the remains of what must have been a bus much like ours. The driver of that vehicle was much less careful than he, our driver reassured me. After that I decided it was time to close my eyes and go to sleep.

At the beginning of the following term my fellow students and I used our new, improved language skills to regale our Spanish language tutor with tales of our foreign travels. When my turn came, everyone began to laugh. The Capetillo family would have been proud to hear me. I had lost my lisp – and acquired a real Mexican accent.

In 1975, no aircraft was consistently capable of flying nonstop between the UK and California; Cathy Packe's flight stopped in Ottawa to refuel. Today, there are nine daily nonstops between Heathrow and Los Angeles alone.

FREAK SHOW IN NEPAL, 1977

This mountain kingdom was a haven for hippies in the 70s, says Phil Reeves. But is the party over?

The first and only time my head has actually felt round – and by that I mean completely three-dimensional from the inside – was in a wooden shack on the Tibetan border a quarter of a century ago. It was the era of James Callaghan and Jimmy Carter. Elvis was alive, just. Mao Tse-tung had recently died. We were young, pretentious and, hey, Finding Ourselves.

The 3D tingling inside my skull spread to my tongue, toes, elbows and ears. Exactly why this was so hilarious was never afterwards clear. But it brought on giggles of such intensity that I had to stagger outside into the mud to recover.

Gulping the fresh Himalayan air, eyes watering, I looked blearily up the valley towards the watchtowers and stark new concrete buildings where China's border guards blocked the path to Tibet. Only a few hundred yards of woodland separated our little hash party from certain imprisonment.

We were part of an army of British students and acne-spangled kids in the 'gap year' who every summer picked up their copies of *Middlemarch* and set off eastwards on a mission of self-discovery, mingling on the way with a tide of other European youngsters. Another rucksack-humping army of Antipodeans flooded westwards, determined to explore the world before settling into the good life in Sydney.

Drifting erratically amid this two-way traffic were thousands of hippies who had rejected Western consumerism, capitalism and draconian drug laws in favour of hanging out indefinitely in the Third World's more tolerant and cheap spots. Everyone eventually ended up in Nepal. And everyone, including the somewhat puzzled Nepalese, called the hippies 'freaks'.

In January 2003, I returned to Kathmandu for the first time. My mission was to cover the latest instalment of the brutal six-year 'People's War' between Maoists and the government that has cost some 8,000 lives. The current monarch, King Gyanendra, took power after the crown prince drunkenly massacred much of the royal family in June 2001, before killing himself.

Two days after my arrival, a ceasefire was unexpectedly declared. Nepal's mightily abused and overwhelmingly poor 23 million people were able at last to have a break from the tyranny of conflict and systematic abuse, albeit probably short-lived.

So there was time to search the clogged-up human warren that is Kathmandu for the scuff marks of Western itinerants who – for all the current rhetoric about the frontier-breaking Internet and the new global village – were able to range more freely 26 years ago than their contemporary counterparts.

The combination of global insecurity post-September 11, south Asia's regional instability and the Maoists has done great damage to Nepal's tourist industry. The music of Deep Purple and Led Zeppelin still coils out of the near-empty bars and cafés of Thamel, a network of alleys cluttered with trekking agencies, money changers, Internet cafés and shops advertising Ayurvedic massages. It is still pleasingly bizarre: 5 hours 45 minutes ahead of GMT (asserting its separation from India by being 15 minutes ahead). This is the year 2059 (they use a lunar calendar).

Marijuana is banned, but available. Pushers and pimps occasionally sidle up with whispered offers of drugs or women. Yet for now the party seemed to be over. But for a

133

handful of casinos in the posh hotels, I found that the place shut for business at 10.30 p.m.

In the 70s, Kathmandu was a haven. It was a major destination for the 'Magic Bus' that lurched back and forth across Asia, packed with hairy youngsters, defiant in its multicolour livery, oblivious to the conservative sentiments of the inhabitants whose landscape it was traversing. It was a rat-infested oasis of cheap cafés, free love, and $1-a-night flophouses where the seriously cool could sit around munching buttered toast and mourning Jim Morrison without fear of ridicule. Hash cookies were sold in the shops.

Dope was very, very cheap. Even so, I can remember coming across young Westerners who, though guests in one of the world's poorest nations, were busking. The memory of one mud-caked and emaciated cockney squatting on the pavement, naked but for a grubby loincloth, has stuck with me. He had a little copper collection pot by his side, and long matted hair, like a Hindu 'sadhu', a holy man. But he was simply begging. I don't know whether anyone gave him much: most young travellers tended to be fantastically stingy, haggling over tiny sums. We made the worst tourists.

'All that hippie stuff is finished now,' said Chandan Shrestha, 45, proprietor of what was once a popular hippie hostel, The Traveller's Paradise Hotel just off Durbar Square, a cluster of impressive-looking temples which forms the centre of Old Kathmandu. 'There were so many hippies that some of them ended up sleeping in the streets. They used to beg from each other. Every other shop sold hash. Now those places are all cybercafés.'

Nepal – fed up with the junkies – banned hashish in the early years of the late King Birendra; the following night, perhaps in protest, one of the city's largest palaces was burned down.

Our little group fell into the most earnest of the category of travellers to Nepal (after the depressingly worthy mountain trekkers): we were first-year university students on holiday. Within our ranks, there were occasional touches of Hippie-Lite: baggy cotton smocks and a splash or two of tie-dye, subconscious attempts not to alienate the freaks in case they automatically chalked us up as tossers. To my young eyes, they seemed rather impressive.

Our expedition included Alison Cahn, who went on to become a TV documentary maker; Pauline Boerma, now an international environmental consultant; and Andrew Tyrie, who has been Conservative MP for Chichester since 1997. I do not intend to further Mr Tyrie's political career by suggesting that he inhaled, or indeed went anywhere near the chunky-looking joint which had overwhelmed me in the hut; he behaved impeccably, like a man who already knew that public life lay ahead.

In fact, that particular spliff belonged to a wild-eyed pig-tailed American whom we had encountered on the road and who had invited me to spend an afternoon helping polish off his sizeable supply of hashish before taking the country bus back to Kathmandu. The American was the real thing, a copper-bottomed, brass-necked, steel-nerved freak, a member of a species now almost as hard to find in Nepal as the yeti.

But they have at least been immortalised in name: Freak Street is just off Durbar Square. You can still buy cloth tie-dye shoulder bags, bead purses, sagging long-sleeved muslin T-shirts and brilliantly coloured bandanas. 'Some freakies still come here,' said Hari Sharan Bhetwal, the 24-year-old proprietor of The Freak Street Trade and Export shop, gazing forlornly down the near-deserted street in search of clients. 'We still get one or two, but not many.'

Although down, they are not out. Across the road, the smell of fresh paint wafts out of the Yellow House Lodge, a dingy $2-a-night Freak Street dosshouse. The proprietor, Jadgi Shawdr, 24, has been decorating. Giant crimson and cadmium-yellow flowers have appeared on the damp ochre-coloured walls. So have a flame-throwing psychedelic dragon's face, the word 'Peace' in large letters, and – oh, joy! – the old ban-the-bomb logo.

The hippies will be back one day, Jadgi explains happily; he wants to be ready. He is planning to hold jamming sessions with his electric guitar; he can play 'Stairway To Heaven'. He certainly looks the part – goatee, pigtails, worn-out jeans – although he says he does not smoke dope any more.

'It is really good to be a hippie, like, happy, man. They have freedom, no stress. They can go anywhere and, like, just survive.' Right now, he says, Nepal has 'all this political bullshit' to contend with. 'It's also really tight over here for the hashish. If the police see you smoking, they put you in jail for six months.' I nodded and thanked him and began to leave. Even in our farewells, he had history down to a T. 'Bye! Stay cool! Peace!' he cried. For a brief and happy moment, my head felt three-dimensional again.

On 27 March 1977, 574 people died in the worst-ever air disaster, when Boeing 747s belonging to Pan Am and KLM collided on the runway at Los Rodeos airport in Tenerife.

TEMPEST IN TORRIGLIA, 1978

Rhythm sticks, boisterous adolescents and a whiff of Pesto remind Philippa Goodrich of a summer that brought the first stirrings of romance.

Summer 1978: the era of Ian Dury and the Blockheads, the year Aldo Moro was kidnapped and killed by the Red Brigades, and the year of my first trip abroad. I was longing to go. Most of my friends from the well-heeled world of Sevenoaks in Kent had been going on skiing holidays or trips to Spain since they were tiny. But I was fifteen and I'd never even been on a ferry to France, let alone on an aeroplane to somewhere more exotic. At last my moment had come. I could hardly believe it but I was to go to Milan for two weeks on an exchange with an Italian girl called Silvia.

The trip didn't start auspiciously – we arrived at Gatwick, only to find that the baggage handlers were on strike and we would have to wait for twelve hours. I can't remember now if we went home or not, but I do remember not being unduly deterred by it. So novel was the whole experience that striking up conversation with a Texan who had already waited longer than us, or gazing round the departure lounge at the prostrate bodies of fellow travellers trying to sleep away the tedium was all part of the adventure.

When we arrived in Milan – almost a day late by now – I was overwhelmed by the strangeness of it all. Silvia lived in a flat. That was odd for a start. Being a clergy child I'd only ever lived in rather large and well-worn vicarages. Silvia had no siblings, so this flat was quiet, odd as well for someone from a family of four daughters. It had marble floors, rooms that were only used on Sundays and kept in semi-darkness for the rest of the week, and a front door that had a layer of steel in the middle and a bolt that clicked smartly into place after you'd turned the key five times. It had a clean and slightly pungent smell of pasta, pesto and herbs that are familiar to me now, but were unknown then.

Silvia had a mother called Franca who – and this to me was the most peculiar thing of all – changed from a flowered house wrap to an expensive linen dress just to go to the supermarket five blocks of flats down the road. Suddenly the novelty was too much and I was very homesick. I can remember swallowing hard to keep the tears at bay on the roof of Milan's famous cathedral on one of the many outings that Silvia and Franca kindly took me on, and when I rang home I couldn't speak in case sobs came out instead of my voice.

Salvation came when they took me on a trip out of Milan to a small town called Torriglia in the mountains behind Genoa. Suddenly we were in the midst of noisy, technicolour, rude, raw Italy. 'Hit me with your rhythm stick' accompanied us wherever we went. We fell in with a group of girls and boys our own age who came up there every summer from Genoa. To me they seemed wild and exotic creatures. Everything about their lives was different from mine. Girls and boys mixed easily together (amazing for someone from an all-girl family and a girls' school to observe) and went in and out of favour with each other from one day to the next. Parents were nowhere to be seen and they roamed as freely as they liked. Even when they went to church on Sunday they didn't stand up and sit down for an hour at the behest of a beady-eyed incumbent, but wandered in and out of the church at will.

The main thing was they didn't know the meaning of the words shy or reserved, and within hours of our first meeting

I had been firmly befriended by Cristina, the smallest, darkest and liveliest girl in the group. She practised her (very impressive) English on me, and I learned my first few Italian words and developed a passion for Italian pop music. I think Silvia, a Milanese convent girl, felt slightly dubious about this boisterous crowd from the wrong end of the Ligurian coast, but all I wanted to do was hang out with them. I thought the day wasted if we hadn't managed to run into them at least twice.

The boy I developed a serious crush on was Alessandro. He had dark curly hair and a moody expression and I only ever managed to blurt out about two words to him. He didn't reckon to talk too much himself, which of course just made him more mysterious and therefore more desirable. All of a sudden, Ian Dury was replaced by Umberto Tozzi, a fully paid-up Italian crooner, and his romantic hit 'Tu'. The song had just the right touch of longing and against this musical background I admired Alessandro from afar until the day Cristina and her friends rumbled me – probably after I'd asked in a nonchalant fashion where he was.

'Oh, Philippa likes Alessandro,' they choroused. This was too much. In the litany of dire, blush-making situations, having it made public that you liked someone came pretty near the top. I had no choice but to issue an instant and categorical denial, and to give my denial credibility I devoted myself for the rest of the holiday to the most short-back-and-sides, un-Italian, unthreatening boy in the group. My love affair with a real-live member of the opposite sex might not have got off the ground, but a longer-lasting love of Italy and its language is rooted in that summer. I went on to study Italian at university because of that holiday. And though the love might have been diluted as other countries have joined the favourites list, it's never been eclipsed. And I can still sing the first three lines of 'Tu' and have a stab at the chorus.

In summer 1978, a charter flight from Gatwick to Milan cost around £150. In summer 2004, a scheduled flight on the route with easyJet is available for around £120.

COO-EE OVER THE MOUNTAIN, 1979

Released from her stuffy British boarding school, Siobhan
Mulholland found magic up Mount Mulanje.

I don't think you ever forget climbing your first mountain.
Mine was Mount Mulanje in southern Malawi. The fact that
it's the only mountain I've ever climbed is probably why I
remember it so well: I have no other 'mountaineering'
experience to confuse it with. Mulanje is a big mountain, one
of the highest in southern Africa, but it's actually not that
difficult to conquer. It's more of a hike than a climb.
However, the technicalities of getting to the top of a
mountain are not why I remember my summer of '79 – it's
more to do with the awesome surroundings I was in, the
people I was with, and the age I was at: fourteen.

At the time, my parents were living and working in
Lilongwe, the capital of Malawi. I had been released from my
austere English boarding school for the summer. Like most
expatriate kids, my Malawian holidays followed a privileged
and relatively tame timetable; hanging out by the pool,
playing tennis, spending weekends by Lake Malawi and,
occasionally, visiting a game park.

Most excursions could be achieved with some comfort,
which suited my family who were definitely not hardy
outdoor types. We never roughed it; we didn't do sturdy
boots, sleeping bags or rucksacks. So when a couple of more
robust families invited my brother and me to join an
expedition up Mount Mulanje it sounded very alternative.
Our fellow climbers were from the British High Commission:
Mr and Mrs Evans and their four teenagers; and Mrs

Stephens and her four plus their German foreign exchange student. (Bit of a coup, that, I thought, getting an exchange to Central Africa rather than Surrey.) I didn't really know the families Evans or Stephens; I might have bumped into them at the Club or the High Commissioner's Christmas party, but you have to understand that in the 70s in Lilongwe shopping malls, cinema outings and slumber parties were not part of the teenage expat agenda. However, being the child of parents who spent their working lives in foreign postings, I became socially very agile. You needed to be: that summer I was one of ten pasty-faced teenagers from bleak British boarding schools let loose up an African mountainside.

It was all terribly well organised. Each member of the party was given an itinerary of the trip and a list of things to take. What clothes to pack was for me the most difficult. In 1979 Malawi was a one-party state under the dictatorial rule of 'President for Life' Dr Hastings Kamuzu Banda. He allowed no opposition or dissent; those who put their heads above the parapet were imprisoned or killed. The draconian laws he imposed on his country, one of the poorest in the world, varied from the misplaced and cruel to the totally bizarre. At the bizarre end was Banda's big hang-up about 70s fashion; men were not allowed to wear flared trousers or have long hair – it had to be cut above the collar. Women were not allowed to wear miniskirts, shorts or trousers, only skirts that covered their knees. This posed a real problem for me on my first expedition – after all, how many women have you seen climbing mountains in below-the-knee A-line skirts? Banda's dictates did nothing to help a self-conscious teenager's agony over which T-shirt would go with which sartorially tragic skirt.

The only way to Mulanje from Lilongwe was by road, via the M1. Unlike its namesake in Britain, this was a badly potholed single lane, running from the north of the country to the south. What you didn't want to do is what we did: get stuck behind a lorry for most of the way and have to sit in the back of a 1970s British Leyland Land Rover. I doubt they make them as uncomfortable as that anymore. We stopped several times: to let cattle cross, change a tyre, look at wood carvings being sold at the roadside, and allow a couple of funeral processions to pass. Wherever we stopped, even if there were no village or huts in sight, Malawian children would appear and chat away. You couldn't rush a trip like this; we were in an amiable mellow country and our drive reflected this.

My fellow mountaineers and I met up at a tea-planters house at the base of the mountain. Here we were introduced to our porters – like all Malawians they were friendly and courteous and, I found, happy to keep their distance. From here we were taken to our starting point in the back of a lorry. What followed was a surprising, and at times, surreal five days. Mulanje is a big mountain, covering an area of 600 square kilometres. It's also steep – rising dramatically from an undulating plain below. Locally it's known as the 'Island in the Sky', because most of its peaks soar up above the clouds. The highest peak is Sapitwa at 3001 metres. However, for beginners Mulanje is a treat of a mountain; you don't need to be a rock climber to reach most summits and you can walk from one side to the other.

We spent five days crossing the Mulanje Massif. Only day one was arduous: a four-hour ascent to the plateau. Any views to be had were covered in mist, drizzle dampened our spirits and clothes throughout our climb, and my feet hurt in my borrowed boots. But once on the plateau the weather cleared, the sun came out and from then on we had the most desirable weather any hiker could ask for: cool, clear and sunny. This was the middle of Malawi's dry season, when the country's climate is at its best.

I was awed by the elemental beauty of Mulanje; deep valleys, gentle plateaus, waterfalls, rock pools, the extreme contrasts of barren rock and lush vegetation. The light up there was amazing – everything was much brighter and clearer. But most of all I remember the wonderful feeling of being alone; the odd bird circling, cloud drifting by, or breeze blowing and that was it. The silence was stunning. The only sign that anyone had been there before was the network of winding footpaths. There was no rubbish any-where, no debris, and no hint of others. Each day we walked three to six hours to a different rest house. It was a gentle trek; the porters did all the hard work. A predictable order appeared in our party. The boys strode ahead with the girls bringing up the rear. If the distance between the two became too much Mrs Stephens would yodel 'coo-ee' across the mountain in a voice similar to Margo from *The Good Life*; a surreal sound in such African isolation.

I surprised myself, and my fellow mountaineers, by being able to keep up with the boys, and occasionally overtaking a few of them. In fact I became as competitive as the boys, if not more so. In hindsight I think this was a gauche attempt by a girl in a single-sex school to attract male attention. (I did in time, learn to nurture my more vulnerable side, realising that physical prowess is not always the best way to attract men.) The rest houses we slept in were basic but clean; wooden huts with bunks, benches and open fires. In the evenings Mrs Evans and Mrs Stephens took it in turns to organise a supper of stew or curry. This was followed by a tin cup of Malawi brandy – lovely at the time but perhaps not the smoothest after-dinner drink. Maybe it was the altitude, maybe the tiredness, maybe my inexperience at drinking brandy, but I found myself having very pubescent thoughts about the Stephens's German exchange student after one of those nightcaps.

I was relieved when the expedition was over. Spending the best part of a week with a group of people you don't really know, in fairly intense circumstances, is hard work. However, if the opportunity arose again I would jump at the chance to visit Malawi and climb Mulanje. Admittedly when I holidayed there times were easier: exports of tobacco and tea were doing well, South African money was coming in, the war in neighbouring Mozambique had not begun, and AIDS was yet to decimate much of this part of Africa. Undoubtedly, for the Malawians life is tragically much tougher now. But for the tourist, I'm told that Malawi is still a paradise to visit, and Mulanje a magical mountain to climb.

12 June 1979: one of the first acts of Margaret Thatcher's new government was to abolish foreign exchange controls, which previously limited the amount of money British travellers could spend abroad.

1980s

ICE CREAMS AND ZEBRAS, 1980

Ska, apple doughnuts and topless ice-cream selling on the French Rivera in 1980 stood Kerri Sharp in good stead for the coming decade, but what did zebras and snorkels have to do with anything?

It was late June 1980. I'd been back in the UK for about six weeks after spending nine months in the mountain wilderness of Crete, eking out a biblical existence tending to goats, picking oranges and making bulrush mats to line the stone dwelling I had inhabited for the best part of three months. Consequently, adjusting back to life in Hackney was never going to be easy, especially for a born-again nature girl who could now add 'shepherdess' to her CV at the tender age of nineteen.

I returned to a Britain with a Conservative female Prime Minister at the helm, and the air – if not yet the winter – tense with discontent. Inner-city riots were just around the corner, and I sensed tough times were heading my way, despite the excitement of a new magazine called *The Face* hitting the newsstands and the two-tone sound of the Specials and the Beat livening up the student parties I'd gate-crashed since my return. It was the last year of my teenage decade and I was yet to work out where I would live and what I would do with my life. In order to postpone being funnelled into making any kind of responsible decision, I keenly accepted the chance to accompany my great friend and heartthrob of the time, Will Webster, to France, to spend the second half of the summer picking grapes or something equally idyllic that I naively assumed would bring us closer together.

I cashed in the last of my National Savings Certificates and we headed onto the night ferry at Newhaven, bound for Dieppe. From there it was thumbs out all the way to the village of Cogolin in Provence, where, Will had been informed, fruit-picking jobs with stout meals thrown in awaited young English folk prepared to get their hands dirty. Except we were about six weeks too early. After spending a few nights sleeping in vineyards and waking up 'boiled in the bag', fast running out of francs, we took the advice of other itinerant workers and headed to the south coast – where we were casually told we could find work selling ice creams on a beach down the road from St Tropez.

St Tropez! The French Riviera! Blimey, we would land on our feet after all. The very name St Tropez was loaded with decadent significance, promising all that was chic and happening. We would hang out and discuss literature and art and smoke toasted cigarettes and try to spot Mick Jagger. Culturally, it was a long way from tending goats and I felt very pleased with myself for packing my bottle of *Rive Gauche* along with my monkey boots. St Tropez famously does not have a beach, and 'just down the road' turned out to be Cavalière, part of a larger and duller coastal area known as Le Lavandou. In 1980, this was a seaside resort for the comfortably wealthy, but there was nothing very chic going on. The avant-garde, if they had ever visited at all, had long since moved on.

The huge stretch of sand at Cavalière was hugged by a winding coastal road with large, gracious houses set back in shaded grounds – a retreat of verandas, tea lawns, conservatories and fountains. The place reeked of affluence. Our home for the next six weeks would reek of many things but, unfortunately, affluence played no part. Our funds allowed us only one choice: tucked a good two miles inland was a barren scrubland with sparse amenities that had the temerity to call itself a campsite. It certainly wasn't luxury, but it was where the other British summer workers pitched up for the duration, and the banter was self-deprecating and pessimistic – just how we liked it. Long-stay campers at Daktari's – as the place was affectionately named, for reasons that would soon become apparent – had a number of conditions imposed on them: no fires, no dogs, no radios, no parties, no rowdy behaviour, no sexual misconduct.

These rules were read out to us on arrival by the campsite owner, who stood sentry at the gates during the day, leaving his post only to poke around the camp in the afternoon to check on tidiness of tents when the inhabitants were at work. With the build and temperament of Basil Fawlty at his most fractious – complete with khaki shorts that billowed over gristly knees like an extra from *It Ain't Half Hot, Mum* – he cut a comedic yet imposing dash, and his barely concealed loathing for rock'n'roll rascals like us made for some impressive facial tics.

The only square of land left for us to pitch on was next to a huge bivvy occupied by about twelve ex-public schoolboys on their gap year, with all the guffawing and blowing off that one can imagine from such a party. In this era of lightweight, hi-tech camping kit, built-in groundsheets and Gore-Tex flaps, it's hard to imagine that only a generation ago such inventions were but the twinkle in an inventor's eye. Here we had a bunch of chaps all bunking down together under the canvas of an old ridge tent that looked as if it had jumped right off the Camp Coffee label. It doubtless hadn't seen the light of day since one of their ex-wing commander dads had brought it down from his loft and dusted it off, announcing that it had stood him in good stead against Rommel.

Rommel seemed like a cheery prospect in comparison with our own camp Kommandant, who, not content with 'inspecting' our enclave during the day, also seemed to relish night patrol, where he would seek out campers who were having anything like a jolly time of things, and berate them in heavily accented English. Thrashing his night stick around and bellowing 'Silence' in an increasingly manic timbre, he would ritually work himself into a terrible lather should any of us attempt to turn the radio up beyond the '4' position. I hate to think what he would have done if he had witnessed any sexual misconduct. Still, his intolerance proved to be a bonding device for cementing good-neighbour relations with the toffs next door – who insisted on the radio thing, but all it ever seemed to play was 'Funky Town' by Lips Inc. – *the* Europop hit of the summer.

Selling ice cream on the beach sounded like a workshy fop's dream job. Until, that is, the miserable reality kicked in on the first day when an odious git named Richard arrived to drop off our supplies and impart the wisdom of his sales technique. He had somehow got a sneak preview of the corporate chest-thumping that was to sweep the 80s, and we were all given embarrassing affirmations to chant of how 'Team DCI are the winners. What are we?' beside the road. This gainful employment involved lugging a cool-box packed with dry ice (which weighed about 10kg) up and down the soft sand of Cavalière beach for some seven hours per day yelling out, '*demandez de glace*' and '*beignet aux pommes*', in the vain hope that one or two of the brittle, lizard-skinned sun-worshippers who populated the beach would suddenly be interested in ramming Wall's Cornettos or apple doughnuts down their necks. This from a species who looked as if nothing more calorific than a *citron pressé* and a light salad had ever passed their lips. Blackpool it was not.

Team DCI vendors received one franc (10p) for every ice cream sold, and 50 centimes (5p) for every apple doughnut. Such were our 'wages'. Will had erred on the optimistic side of miscalculation when being given the job, thinking we got 10F (£1). This would have been just about tolerable if we had the place to ourselves. As it was, we were two of approximately thirty young vendors from rival companies who operated the half-mile patch. Unsightly squabbles for turf erupted every day and only the wiliest earned enough to eat *and* pay their camp charges.

But we were just outside St Tropez, I kept thinking. And it couldn't be that bad, could it? Maybe not if you had a back pocket stuffed with traveller's cheques. If you had to earn a living from manual labour, things were not so rosy. On top of this, carrying the apple doughnuts provided the extra challenge of ensuring that they remained sand-free. All in all, it was a tall order.

If you walked along the flat, cooler part of the beach for some relief from the scorching sun, you missed potential customers as it was too far away from the sun-loungers; if you trudged through the superfine powder nearer to your uninterested clientele, you would build calf muscles like Arnie in his heyday within a week – with all the aches and pains that accompanies such a pursuit. After two days of this, I felt more like Roy Kinnear in *The Hill* rather than the carefree 'Jane Birkin wrapped in silk sarong' reverie that I had so lucidly cultivated.

There was also the problem of sun glare. Having lost my sunglasses on my first day I was hopeless and helpless. Squinting into the noonday French sun in August while on the trudge with the icebox was no picnic. When one day I found a discarded cheap pair of round 'John Lennon' shades, I was gleeful, only to be told by Will that they made me 'look so odd I would scare customers away'. A worse countenance than squinting and pissed off? It must have been bad. I was crestfallen.

There was only one solution. My secret ammo: the 'girls' would have to make an appearance. If I had to go *sans lunettes de soleil*, I was also going to go *sans bikini top*. Despite the fact that every other female bar the ice-cream vendors was topless (still a rare sight to English eyes in 1980), using such burlesque tactics while engaged in one's daily toil still felt a little, well, inappropriate. But it seemed to work a treat. I didn't need a degree in logic to realise that an upturn in my day's takings to 50F (five whole pounds) might have been due to my following a long and saucy British tradition of getting them out for the garçons. That night around the campfire with the Etonians, a better class of wine was enjoyed, and countless hectic games of charades.

You wake up early in the Gallic August heat, and many were the times that the day kicked off with a hangover. It was such a morning that I was exposed to a particularly memorable event: one I'll wager to be in the top ten of curious sights of camping history. I was making my way to the washrooms when suddenly a zebra turned the corner at a fair old trot, followed swiftly by a very, very short, rotund man wearing a mask and snorkel and holding a length of rope – that I presumed had until recently been connected to the zebra. I instantly reprimanded myself for declining my mother's advice to pack her Victorian French/English phrasebook, wherein lurked such useful sentences as: 'Excuse me, but your zebra has cast off its snorkel', but before I had time to reflect on this oversight, an almighty roar filled the morning air at the same time as a giraffe's head went up-periscope from behind the eucalyptus trees.

Having spent camping trips in the New Forest and North Wales, I was used to seeing the odd horse or cow in the meadow come time for the eggs & b., but this was most irregular. Lions? Dwarves? Only in Kamp Daktari would hospitality be offered to a Yugoslavian gypsy circus troupe. Kamp Kommandant had a heart after all. Or maybe just a sick sense of humour.

I got used to walking past the caged lion of an evening, en route to the wine shop, and it was only after we left the campsite that the delightful incongruity of a circus by the sea began to impinge onto my imagination like a story by Angela Carter. At the time, after the initial shock, it seemed so natural, and I confess to worrying perhaps too earnestly about animal welfare when it was Will and I who were starving and being cruelly treated.

Still, after three weeks of toil we were leaner, healthier and sporting an impressive colour, despite having a financial crisis at least once every day. In the noonday sun, when it was too hot, we played dominoes and read from our respective American beat novels. There were minor crises, however. I caught an ear infection and went totally deaf for two days, unable to afford any medication; I wondered if I'd ever hear 'Funky Town' again. There was the day I was inconsolable on hearing that Peter Sellers had died, and the time I bravely ventured to the nudist beach further up the coast road, and got into a sticky situation with a Cornetto and an angry German. Will took things at a more leisurely pace than I, although he suffered a terrible bout of ennui that lasted several days after I tried to involve him in a beach volleyball tournament.

My twentieth birthday was spent working as usual. I didn't do very well for presents that year, although Will gave me his by-then battered copy of a Jack Kerouac biography and a fab

Polish guy called Witek bought me a packet of sweet peanuts. I believe that lunch consisted of the usual hard-boiled egg and stolen apple doughnut.

September was soon under way and it was time to return to England. When we told the Etonians we were off, the lads went into a military huddle and came back with The Plan. We were bundled into their battered 2CV and driven out under cover of night, giving Daktari the slip, thereby saving us enough money to have a not-too-badly off hitchhike back to the UK. We hadn't dreamed of not paying, but the chaps thought it would be a bit of a wheeze to 'get one back at the old bugger'. We laughed all the way to Lyon.

Will was off to Loughborough for his MA in American Literature. Witek returned to Poland to join the burgeoning *Solidarnosc* movement and I returned to London. I found it as hard to adjust to urban life then as I had two month's previously. In order to squeeze my year of living outdoors for as long as I could, I even pitched my tent for a couple of weeks at the Crystal Palace campsite, just under the television mast. But the summer was over and I had to finally face adulthood and a decade of parties where a shocking amount of illegal substances would be imbibed. But whatever passed my lips, I have never again – in any state of inebriation – encountered a zebra being chased by a dwarf wearing a mask and snorkel.

Crystal Palace Camp Site, London SE19, is still going, and opens each year March to October. Tel: 020 8803 6900. Fax: 020 8676 0980. Pitches: 60.

THE ALDERNEY FILES, 1980

Lucy Gillmore fondly recalls halcyon days, scratchy jumpers and great-uncle Maurice's crab sandwiches.

My great-uncle Maurice almost killed me reversing off the harbour wall in Alderney. I was ten. A three-point turn at the end of the breakwater went slightly wrong and one of the wheels spun crazily over the edge. Uncle Maurice was an ex-army major turned hot-tempered chef, who didn't like little girls whining. So I bit my lip as ten sausage dogs crawled all over me barking hysterically, and he manoeuvred us back on to dry land.

Alderney, the islanders laugh, is often called the Cinderella of the Channel Islands. It's not, they tell you, because she's beautiful and poor, but because she has two ugly big sisters. Jersey and Guernsey probably don't find it quite so amusing. The island is three and a half miles long by one and a half wide and only eight miles from the Normandy coast. And it is beautiful, with cliffs covered in wild flowers, white sandy beaches and a turquoise sea. The narrow cobbled streets of the little town of St Anne are lined with pastel-coloured Georgian houses and whitewashed stone terraces. It is also the least visited of the main Channel Islands; a little backwater that has escaped mainstream tourism. It's sleepy and sort-of-French – and it's the place where I spent my childhood holidays.

Uncle Maurice is an Alderney legend. First he ran the Marais Hall pub in the cobbled market square where auctions for the now extinct Alderney cow (slightly smaller than the Guernsey) were once held. My brother and I would play in the old cattle trough in front of the pub. Next he renovated the Old Barn near Loungis Common, which became the island's first upmarket restaurant. Uncle Maurice's final project was to turn the old 'caff' on the harbour into The First and Last to catch the yachting trade. It's still renowned on both sides of the Channel for its seafood.

Holidays revolved around my uncle's cooking – crab crepes, crab salad, crab bisque and crab sandwiches. And the beach. Everyday my father would walk outside our holiday cottage, lick his finger, and hold it up to judge which way the wind was blowing. Then we'd head for whichever of Alderney's golden beaches he decreed would be the most sheltered. Braye had nasty little black flies. Corblets had the biggest waves. Loungis, with its long concrete wall built by prisoners of war during the German occupation, was a bit austere. Saye was my mother's favourite. A beautiful horse-shoe bay lined by grassy dunes with fine white sand and a calm sea.

Sitting in Southampton airport again fifteen years later (my uncle had died some years before), I tried to dredge up other memories. I remembered long walks on the cliffs littered with strange German bunkers (Alderney was evacuated in 1940 and occupied by the Germans for five years) and vivid blue cornflowers, crying over itchy Guernsey jumpers and rabbits dying from myxomatosis. And my uncle's dogs. They all had German names except for old Murphy. Gretel was the runt and silky little Heidi the favourite. They sat on his shoulder and drank beer from his pint glass. The frothy head stuck to his moustache as he kissed them on the mouth. Auntie Rita would hug us to her ample bosom, her make-up always perfect, her hair coiffeured and her voice tinkling. Auntie Rita is still there, an institution on the island, running The First and Last. As the yachtsmen set sail they make a note to call the harbourmaster and Rita with their ETA – not necessarily in that order. The planes are the same too; still way too small and canary yellow. Aurigny's Trilanders take up to fifteen people. Dogs go half price and get their own seat. Strapped in beside a muzzled Jack Russell, freight piled into the empty seats behind, we roared down the runway.

'The Channel Islands don't belong to the UK you know. The UK belongs to the Channel Islands.' I was taking a quick island tour with Bob to help me put the pieces together.

'William the Conqueror was the Duke of Normandy,' he explained, enjoying my look of bewilderment. 'When he conquered England and took the crown, he gave up most of his lands but kept the Channel Islands. So the English Crown belongs to the Duchy of Normandy.' To this day, the Queen is the Duke of Normandy. 'That's Ian Botham's house over there. Laura Ashley and the woman who created the Wombles, Lisa Beresford, lived here too. The last Womble is called Alderney. And there's the Old Nunnery,' Bob added. The nuns never lived there. It was the German whorehouse. That Alderney sense of humour again.

Alderney is an island with attitude. Tourists are called visitors and an aristocrat sweeps the streets. Spurning the G&T set, he needed a reason to get up in the mornings, but the only job going was as a road sweeper. So he took it. 'There's the President.' Bob pointed to a grey-haired man driving a battered old Ford Sierra. Walking along the cliffs looking out towards Gannet Rock, hundreds of birds circling above the crashing waves, I passed an enormous concrete gun installation. The ground around it was carpeted with cornflowers and clover scenting the salty air.

Some people find Alderney boring. They say that there's nothing to do. But part of its appeal is that it's in a time warp. The cinema only has showings on Thursdays and Mondays.

Shops still close half-day on Wednesday and all day Sunday. Nobody locks their doors or their cars. The bobbies sent over from Guernsey either view their stint on Alderney as a holiday or a punishment. When more and more people are looking for the ultimate escape, it seems odd that they miss a world-apart on their doorsteps.

And there's history of course. There have been settlements on Alderney since Neolithic times. The island has been called the Fortress Island and has forts scattered around the coastline from Essex Castle above Loungis, a gift from Elizabeth I to the Earl of Essex, to the forts built during the 19th century to protect the island from the threat of Napoleonic invasion. Nowadays many of the old Victorian forts have been converted into luxury apartments or holiday lets. Fort Tourgis is the next in line. You can stay in Fort Clonque – it's now one of the Landmark Trust's properties, cut off at high tide and decked out with old iron army beds and Victorian furniture. Some of the German bunkers up on the cliffs are even used for raves during the summer.

Wandering around the Alderney Museum, housed in the old school, I read about the Alderney cow, the German occupation and concentration camps and the old cannon dredged up from the wreck of the 16th-century *Makeshift*, said to be more important than the discovery of the *Mary Rose*. And the island's blond hedgehog, originally brought over from Harrods in a shopping bag, or so they say.

I had been worried that the Alderney of my childhood would have disappeared; that it would be somehow diminished and I would find it dull. But not only has it not changed – it is more beautiful and interesting than I remember.

And how often can you say that?

On 25 April 1980, the worst-ever disaster involving a British charter flight took place, when a Boeing 727 belonging to Dan-Air crashes into Mount Teide, Tenerife, after a flight from Manchester. All 146 passengers and crew died. The accident did not lead the evening news in the UK that day, which instead led on the bungled US attempt to rescue the hostages in Tehran.

GREYHOUND BOUND, 1981

Sophie Campbell remembers her rite of passage through the USA.

At 1 a.m. on 3 June 1981, President Reagan had already been shot. So had the Pope. The Soviets were in Afghanistan, Mrs Thatcher was in No. 10 and I was in a bus at LA Greyhound station, in tears.

When I look back at my diary of that month crossing America, it seems hard to believe. Had I really never seen a bar code? Had I honestly not heard of dim sum, or the Grateful Dead? This was before the first space shuttle, before Di and Charles got married, before Aids. This was an eternity ago.

The diary, which is stuffed full of brochures from theme parks and maps of Smalltown, US, annotated in neat, schoolgirly writing, is chiefly interesting for what it leaves out. There in the gaps, like broderie anglaise, lies the story. For instance, it never mentions that I was in tears – LA Greyhound station is not a pretty place at 1 a.m. – or that my school friend Penny (half my size and twice as brave) was the one who got us on to the bus. Instead it goes into lengthy route descriptions (first leg: LA to Yosemite to San Francisco to Vancouver to Banff) and makes lots of pompous eighteen-year-old observations about Americans.

Some bits I remember well. Such as trying to hang our food up trees because of the bears and never being able to get it down again (there are probably carrier bags full of boloney sandwiches and string cheese dangling from pine trees in Yosemite to this day). Such as falling into the river in the Canadian Rockies while trying to fill up a kettle, and putting hot rocks in my sleeping-bag to try to get warm (it didn't work), and the first guy we hitched a lift from giving us a lecture on why girls shouldn't hitch alone in the States.

Things really came alive when we met Al and Ken, deadheads from New Orleans who had been out west and were heading home on our bus. They, too, told us we shouldn't hitch, so we broke all our own rules and split up, boy–girl, boy–girl, in order to hitch into Yellowstone Park. It snowed six inches that night, not bad for June, and the 'hot pots' (as Al and Ken called the bubbling geysers) pumped steam up into a blizzard. The bar in Gardiner was full of huge, pissed beardies, like the cast of an American road movie, who warned us about grizzlies, guns and hitching. 'Big Grizz!' one of them kept slurring, chequered arms held high. 'Big Grizz could take your head off, like that.'

We found a college friend of Al and Ken's working in the park, stayed illegally in the men's dorm, ate nature burgers (organic food? What was that?) and learned all about Jerry Garcia. Then, we got back on to the bus for a three-day stint from Salt Lake City to Norfolk, Virginia, entering that twilight zone of travel known only to Greyhound users.

They haven't changed much, Greyhounds. I went on one recently and it still made me feel poor. People on long-haul bus rides are people who can't afford domestic flights – and that, in America, is poor. So you get hauled out in the middle of the night to change buses or cross borders, and the lockers are never big enough for a pack, and the seats are never big enough for a human being – especially not for a Floridan or a Texan.

We stayed with friends in Norfolk and then moved on to Washington. People sat in rows in Greyhound stations, watching TV (a quarter for twenty minutes). The same jingles played endlessly on different channels: 'Have a Datsun, it's good for yooooo . . .' I can still hear the tune ringing in my head today.

We detoured to wild, untamed Niagara Falls – or rather, the honeymoon motel capital of the western world – up to Montreal and back down to the States. And after all that, after all those thousands of miles and border crossings and adventures, nemesis chose to present itself in Hartford, Connecticut, one of the most famously boring places in America.

It came in the form of Wazoo – commune dweller and spiker of hash sandwiches – after a hippyish sort of evening running about catching fireflies in jam jars and singing 'The Streets of London' to a guitar.

The sandwiches tasted OK. As first-timers, how were we to know? Until the purple shirts of the band in a local bar shot across the room and wrapped themselves around our eyeballs, and people from long ago and far away began whispering right in our ears.

We had to be taken home and put to bed, like five-year-olds after a family wedding, and listen to guilty hippie whispering insinuate itself under the door. ('You gave them too much.' 'I didn't.' 'You did.') That didn't make the diary, I can tell you. The diary was meant to be about My Trip Across America, not some adolescent rite of passage. Back then, of course, I didn't realise that they were one and the same thing.

In its first summer, 1981, British Leyland's Mini Metro was well on its way to becoming the UK's best-selling car.

LEGLESS IN GEORGIA, 1981

Neil McGowan's request for an avocado got short shrift in Soviet Russia, but his visit did inspire a career change.

I first went to the USSR in 1981 – for all the wrong reasons. I'd gone to a very conventional, even archaic college for my degree, and as a means of annoying my fellow students, friends and family with my choice of vacation destination, the USSR was hard to beat. It was also – although I kept this latter motivation more to myself – incredibly cheap.

I already had half the back of a postage stamp left over from some of my college studies, and I gave this space over unstintingly to my trip planning – which consisted of reading the single sheet of destination information provided by Soviet State monopoly tour-operators Intourist Ltd. The brochure communicated clearly that the USSR was awash with pro- gressive modern cities that were clones of Sheffield, yet populated by groups of smiling girls in national dress who hung around by steel-and-concrete Monuments to Heroism in poses choreographed by Busby Berkeley. My goal of irritating those around me would have been served by any of the Soviet destinations illustrated, so by pinning the tail on the donkey, I found myself aboard an ageing TU-134 at Heathrow headed for a triangular tour of the Caucasus Soviet Republics, via Moscow. It was – with the exception of a helicopter to the Isles of Scilly on a family holiday – my first flight in a plane of any kind.

My chance companions on the trip were disappointingly normal and conformist, as indeed were the inhabitants of Moscow on our whistle-stop transit visit. Was I the only person wearing red glasses east of the Vistula? Dietary preferences among my college friends had been devoted to debating which level of vegetarian asceticism was most worthy – yet here in Socialism Central, requests for meatless meals were met with a disinterested shrug. My carefully practised phrasebook requests for avocado or grapefruit met the same puzzled stares. Red Square, the Kremlin, Lenin's Mausoleum and St Basil's were all closed in preparation for a grandiose State Funeral. We set off instead for a tour of Moscow's B-grade attractions in the command of our state guide and unofficial minder for the experience, Tania.

Tania was a dull and introverted girl who only ever addressed us collectively, by our group reference number. 'Pay attention, Group M-34 – I would like to bring the apartment blocks on our left to your attention, built in the typical 1960s style.' We struggled to distinguish the 1960s ones from their neighbours, making a nice impersonation of the courtiers in *The Emperor's New Clothes*. Enforced collectivisation and bus tours of suburban housing developments? Things were definitely looking up.

The plane in which we flew onwards to Tbilisi was even older than the one from Heathrow, but even before touchdown in the Georgian capital it was becoming clear how different things were from Moscow. 'Hey, let's go for a cigarette at the back,' nudged my Georgian neighbour. It evidently didn't matter that I didn't smoke, although I worried as I went conspiratorially towards the toilet with my new friend that I hadn't planned joining the Mile High Club in a same-sex liaison. 'Change money? Eight for one.'

The rouble had been at parity with sterling at a rate of one-to-one for as long as Marx had been matched with Lenin. 'Eight for one?' I gasped. 'OK, OK, ten for one, best price, yes? Now we drink! Georgian cognac!' I returned to my seat puzzling how it could be so much to his advantage to offer me ten times the bank rate? After several more swigs from the hipflask we landed, and I caught Tania's gaze – which was burning into the back of my neck with full-on Slavic fury.

Our sightseeing programme around Tbilisi was extremely depressing. Every ancient church and monument, every reference to a major Christian kingdom in the 12th century, came as a body blow to my know-it-all sensibilities. By the end of the day I was glum and reticent – how had my much-vaunted education left me in complete ignorance of a whole country of people who had a unique language and alphabet? Moreover, I was a music graduate with pretensions to knowing about 'early stuff' – yet here was elaborate medieval polyphonic choral music, about which I'd never heard a word – and there was still a living tradition of singing it.

My spirits lifted greatly at supper – yes, there were native vegetarian dishes, easily available, and they were, well, delicious. I tucked into the *lobio* bean stew and *khachapuri* cheese breads. Several bottles of local wine later I was standing on my hotel balcony, with steam trains hooting across the luscious warm evening air, watching a forlorn traffic cop trying to referee the machismo-fuelled anarchy rotating in a circular motion around him. My student-age conspiracy-theory paranoia was complete – there really were viable alternatives to the western rat race, with their own languages and food and culture – but they'd been concealed from me by 'the system'. And there on that balcony, fuelled by a litre or so of cheap *kindzmarauli* red wine, I became a latent tour operator. Someone should bring more people to this place! Not just for two to three days, but for full-scale itineraries – and that person could be . . . me?

The next morning we set off by road for Mtskheta – or rather, we gathered in the hotel's parking lot. Unable to sleep, I'd been down early and noticed our driver, Saba, in eager negotiation with a group of Germans – after which some money changed hands, and they drove off with him. After a protracted delay to our departure, Tania appeared from inside the hotel, where she'd been frantically calling. 'There has been a terrible accident. Your driver, Saba, has been killed. Another bus will come in one hour to take us to Mtskheta,' she announced. 'He's not dead – some Germans paid him some cash and he's gone off with them instead,' I ventured, to the great relief of my co-travellers, but to the fury of Tania. 'No-no-no, definitely dead. No other reason for delay, except death of driver. Travel Company Intourist not at fault. We will leave in one hour.' A ramshackle heap with a slipping clutch rolled up, and we set off along the Georgian Military Highway. Mtskheta only confirmed my suspicions – another marvellous place that had been too long concealed. The idea for organising some trips was already buzzing in my head now, and the liberal giveaway material on the Georgian Soviet Socialist Republic in the hotel further prompted my thinking.

Back in Tbilisi that evening we saw Saba very much alive, returning his staggering German customers to the hotel after a day spent tasting in the vineyards. I'd made friends with a gnarled old Australian in the group named Len, and we were setting off for a stroll when some locals approached us, making drink-downing signs and saying 'You come? Yum-yum!' They lived in what appeared to be slums near the hotel. Inside the slums all was palatially decorated with antique furniture, silks and weavings. Our hostess poured us some wine from the barrel, and a ragged multilingual piece of paper translated that we could be served a 'national banket' for $5 each. To this day I've never had better value from five bucks – the food came endlessly, the wine barrel flowed, daughters and sons sang, and the Germans arrived as our fellow guests around the table. We rolled home at about 3 a.m., with a parting plea from our hostess – 'In hotel, not speak!' Next morning, Tania casually pointed out the address as 'primitive slum dwellings – of course, no one lives in such a house now, we have modern houses of sixties construction, which I will show you.'

Beyond one single group, I was never able to recruit any visitors for my self-declared Caucasian paradise. High state-imposed prices put trips beyond the reach of normal mortals, and not long after I was instead leading tours to Russia. The break-up of the USSR could have offered Georgia much – instead, it descended into a civil war that led into a decade of incompetent government. Even the most optimistic travellers were dissuaded by daily electricity outages, the absence of hot water – and sometimes cold too – and acts of random appalling violence. Although I did become a tour operator, Georgian trips have been an idea that's been kept in our deep freeze for nearly ten years. The democratic election in Tbilisi at the start of 2004 could not hope instantly to change the atrophy of years – but I remain hopeful that some time in the next few years, I'll finally be able to run trips to the destination I actually went into the travel business to promote.

Neil McGowan is Managing Director of The Russia Experience (020 8566 8846. www.trans-siberian.co.uk).

The first *Train à Grande Vitesse* (TGV) ran from Paris to Lyon in September 1981, halving the journey time on the 300-mile run to 2 hours, 40 minutes.

A HOSPITAL BED WITH A VIEW, 1984

Smelly wards, awful food, patients left in the corridors. No, not the NHS, says Ian Thomson, but a nightmare in Rome. Still, nice view of the Colosseum, though.

After an unexplained fall, I spent the summer of 1984 in a hospital in Rome. A blurred but familiar face by my bedside divided into three, then two and finally into focus as the English girl who shared my flat on Via Salaria. 'I'm afraid you've had an emergency brain operation,' she said. Then I was out again.

I'd been discovered on the floor of 195 Via Salaria apparently close to death. In best Hitchcock tradition, the telephone was dangling off the hook: the carabinieri thought I'd been coshed. I was 23 years old and newly arrived in Rome to teach English. Bizarrely, I'd been on the phone at the time to the novelist Italo Calvino, whom I hoped to interview. Handprints of blood had covered the walls and congealed in the hall where I lay in a coma. Later, Calvino said he'd heard 'a thud' at my end before the line went dead.

Next day I woke up with a sharp ammonia smell in my nostrils. I was outside a hospital latrine. A sign at the end of the corridor announced: 'Cranial Traumatology Clinic.' A group of nuns swished past, each holding a carafe of white wine. Was I in paradise? The carafes turned out to contain urine samples.

For most Romans, San Giovanni is a nightmare hospital. The wards smell of urine and the food (at least when I was there) was congealed custard and pork gristle, soft and tallowy. Most of the nuns – paramedics – came from the basilica of San Giovanni across the square. In their coifs and black habits they might have been trained in the school of Torquemada. My right arm had gone blue from their injections and I needed their help like a hole in the head.

Surgery for an impacted fracture and resultant haematoma – a swelling composed of blood effused into the tissues of the brain – had in fact left me with a cranial cavity the size of a tangerine. And now, like a bedlamite, I was strapped to a trolley in the corridor. In this scorching August, my surgeons contemplated the fall and (with any luck) rise of their Rome patient.

The chief surgeon was quaintly named Professore Milza – Professor Spleen. With an apologetic smile he cautioned me about my cavity. 'You are missing some bone, my dear Thomson, and therefore less thick-skulled than before.' And he suggested a silver plate to protect my neural circuitry. (For fear of picking up radio signals, however, I decided to opt for a plastic one.)

Following trauma, the brain can rebuild itself in extraordinary ways. My Italian had become unaccountably fluent after the injury. 'Most impressive,' said Professor Spleen, and he raised an eyebrow. 'It's hardly the Berlitz method, but a cranial cavity can certainly work wonders.'

A fortnight into my stay and the men's ward had become so hot that a nurse suggested I sleep on the roof. A makeshift bed was set up for me on the terrace overlooking the Capitoline Hill and Colosseum, where I could enjoy the cool rooftop views and read PG Wodehouse. After three weeks a nun informed me that another haemotoma casualty was on his way, and it was time for me to leave. Bearded and no doubt unrecognisable, I hobbled out into the heat and attempted to hail a taxi. I was recuperating slowly in my Via

Salaria flat when, wedged behind a cupboard, I found an X-ray of the previous occupant showing a fractured skull.

In a fright (had she suffered a blow to the head?) I took the next plane home to London. Shortly after the cranial plate was fitted there I was interviewed for a job. Melvyn Bragg was reading my application when he looked up. 'Good God! What have you done to your head?' I did not get the job. Two decades on, I am still shaken by my brush with mortality that summer of 1984.

Ian Thomson recently won the Royal Society of Literature Heinemann Prize for his biography of Primo Levi.

On 18 July 1984, the UK government sold its cross-Channel ferry operator, Sealink, to Sea Containers Ltd. This Bermuda-based company subsequently sold it on to Stena Line, then took over Britain's Great North Eastern Railway between London and Edinburgh, and the entire Peruvian rail network.

THE SEVEN-YEAR ITCH, 1984

Seven years adrift, Simon Cunliffe returns home to rediscover sunburn, beach cricket, and the brilliant night skies of New Zealand's Golden Bay.

Takaka Hill, towards the northwest tip of New Zealand's South Island, is a forbidding gatekeeper. Its steep hairpins and tortuous S-bends seem designed to discourage the casual traveller, so that by the time you arrive at Harwood Lookout the spirits, like the hang-gliders that sometimes peel and float off the crags above, are eager for a lift. The sight that greets you here is breathtaking: the upper Takaka River valley stretching away towards Golden Bay and Farewell Spit, its patchwork paddocks frequently masked by a misty gauze filtering across from the Tasman mountains beyond. Perhaps light-headed relief comes with the knowledge that it's all downhill from here. But there's something else, too. Entering the Bay you are accosted by a sudden rush of emotion: there is nowhere else in the world quite like it. And nowhere else in the world you'd rather be.

It's 1984. George Orwell's classic has just been made into a movie, this second time with Richard Burton in the role of the inquisitor. Burton himself will not live out the year. JB Priestley has cashed in his chips, as has Truman Capote and poet laureate John Betjeman. Indira Gandhi has been assassinated, and the members of Prime Minister Margaret Thatcher's cabinet have narrowly escaped death at the hands of the IRA in their Brighton hotel. On the other side of the ledger, Prince Harry is born. It's the year of Torvill and Dean, melting hearts and searing the ice with their sizzling Winter

Olympic gold-medal winning performance of *Bolero*. Michael Jackson's *Thriller* has broken all records for album sales, *The Jewel in the Crown* television series has done wonders for British curry houses, and Desmond Tutu has been awarded the Nobel peace prize. Ronald Reagan has been re-elected and in New Zealand, our destination, Labour leader David Lange takes office. His government's radical, far-reaching economic reforms – 'Rogernomics' – have just been initiated.

As we depart for Down Under and a taste of traditional turkey amid sweltering summer temperatures, the sound of Band Aid's charity hit, 'Do They Know It's Christmas?', rings in our ears. I've been gone from the Antipodes since 1977. I'm scratching a seven-year itch. They say this is a critical period for exiles: shall I go or shall I stay? There's plenty of time to ponder the dilemma on the long haul out. We fly Garuda, because it's cheap, and offers a stopover in Bali. We stay a night in Kuta Beach, full of Australian tourists and Balinese hawkers squawking 'Gidday, mate' in broadest ocker accents. Already this resort is fast on the way to becoming the Torremolinos of Southeast Asia. We head north for a few restful days by the sea.

In transit in Sydney, a helpful airline attendant meets my request for window seats, then trumps it: 'View?' says JayJay, with a grin so wide his sun-buffed face threatens to split like a bruised tomato. 'I'll give you a view to make your eyes water.' I had raved about the Southern Alps and wanted to impress my companion on her first visit. Sensing my desperation, JayJay is even better than his word. He upgrades us to business class where we are pampered with crayfish tails and lamb fillets stuffed with spinach and pine nuts, washed down with best Kiwi *méthode champenoise*.

And the homecoming canvas is spectacular: descending through the cumulus to be met by the mountains, their snow-lined jaws and jagged white molars giving way to the vast, quilted Canterbury Plains. We drive north through the guts of the South Island, stopping to idle in the hot pools at Maruia Springs thermal resort, before alighting at the Nelson lakes. We pull on our tramping boots and set off for a walk. On the afternoon of the second day, as we near the summit of Mount Angelus, the weather closes in, summer temperatures plummeting in the face of a southerly assault from Antarctica. Lashed by sleet and gales we crawl, scramble and shiver our way through incipient hypothermia to the hut at the top.

The next day, thoroughly chastened by our narrow escape, we clamber down the mountain and head for Golden Bay. My parents had found the place at a small beach settlement called Parapara the year before. Recently returned from a peripatetic life in Third World development work, they are re-establishing roots. The house is fashioned out of local clay bricks and sits amid ten acres of gorse and scrub with a small pastured paddock or two.

From the lounge and the bedrooms you can see down to the estuary and beyond to the beach. As the tide recedes it reveals a vast acreage of sand. And it is here that we enact all the vital rituals of summer. Not until the first net has been laid on a departing tide in the evening and harvested, all hands on deck, at dawn the following morning does the summer season officially seem open. Never mind that we will spend hours disentangling sand crabs from the netting, plastering fiercely pincered fingers, and stripping the diamond-webbed nylon of seaweed. Occasionally a flatfish or two, a small lemon fish, a snapper will flounder its way into the net, and provide a feed for breakfast.

The beach becomes the site of a marathon cricket series, test match after test match played out against the unhurried rhythms of life without deadlines and meetings and phone calls and, well, trouble. Only the incoming tide intervenes, resetting the boundaries and intermittently sweeping the pitch clean. From Parapara we embark on local journeys of discovery: splashing in freshwater pools up the nearby Aorere Valley; falling down the vertiginous dunes at wild Wharariki beach; four-wheel tripping up the twitcher's paradise of Farewell Spit; and calling in to the rural local – the Mussel Inn – for a chowder and a long cold Pale Whale Ale. At nearby Onekaka we swim with a tame dolphin amid the rotting piles of an old wharf.

In the southern summer of 1984, bathed in Golden Bay's welcoming glow, I recharge the batteries of kith and kinship; I soak up the sun, re-experience the chafing of sand against reddened skin, and begin to feel careless and carefree under the caress of a cooling sea breeze. We marvel, my companion and I, at the scale of the evening sky. Night after night we sit entranced by its brilliant astronomical jewellery. We decide to get married. We promise we will bring our children to this magical place. Ten years later we finally manage to extricate ourselves from London life – and keep our word.

On 22 June 1984, Richard Branson launched the first Virgin Atlantic flight, from Gatwick to Newark, USA. The passengers, many of them journalists travelling free, drank the plane dry by mid-Atlantic.

THEY'LL EAT YOU IN HAITI, 1985

In spite of all the pre-departure horror stories, James Ferguson found a warm welcome amid the poverty and faded elegance.

'Why Haiti, for God's sake? They'll probably eat you at some voodoo ceremony.' My neighbour at the Oxford high-table dinner was puzzled by my choice of academic excursion. I'd applied for a grant to travel to what Graham Greene had unreassuringly dubbed the 'nightmare republic' to pursue my postgraduate research into French history. Amazingly enough, the money was forthcoming, and suddenly the prospect of throbbing drums and headless chickens seemed uncomfortably close.

It was the fault of my girlfriend (now my wife). She'd persuaded me that I would learn more about Toussaint L'Ouverture and the first Black Republic on the spot than in the cloistered safety of the Bodleian Library. We'd survived a short, expensive and very hungry trip to Algeria the year before, so thought that another taste of a former French colony would be instructive, if not exactly fun.

The books I consulted were not encouraging. *The Comedians* isn't a tourist-friendly advertisement, what with Tontons Macoutes, corpses in swimming pools and the like. The Berlitz guide pointed out that in Haiti 'they bury the dead under heavy tombstones to keep them from returning to haunt the living'. A trawl of news cuttings and reports revealed that Baby Doc Duvalier's regime was among the worst human-rights abusers in the Americas.

So, in a state of apprehension, we flew to Jamaica in August 1985, and spent a week or so in Kingston and Port

Antonio, grey, humid and rather decrepit. It was a culture shock of sorts, especially as my experience of abroad, Algeria aside, was limited to France. Jamaica seemed more run down and brooding than exotic.

Nothing, though, could have prepared us for our first impression of Haiti. If the road from Kingston's airport into town goes through some dodgy districts, the way into Port-au-Prince was like shifting a century or two, a snapshot of Third World chaos. There were as many animals as vehicles on a road that was as much pothole as tar. Ramshackle shelters of palm thatch lined the route, interspersed with half-finished breeze-block boxes. Piles of burning rubbish produced a sickly sweet smell that drifted into our antiquated taxi. People were everywhere: children playing in nasty-looking puddles, women squatting by piles of fruit, and everywhere the frenetic and noisy activity of the Haitian capital.

For a terrible moment, it crossed my mind that all of Haiti might be like this. But soon the taxi began to climb into a more salubrious world of high walls and lush gardens, and pulled up outside a large white building of Victorian appearance. This was the Santos guesthouse, an elegant but inexpensive establishment that seemed mostly to cater to the many aid workers who have always been drawn to this land of spectacular poverty.

The Santos, set in the upper-middle-class hillside suburb of Turgeau, promised a retreat of calm and good taste. Stunning Haitian paintings and sculptures complemented mahogany furniture and a cool entrance hall, watched over by the stern but kind Madame Santos. A small pool was shaded by a breadfruit tree. From this haven of *demi-pension* tranquillity we made excursions down into the teeming confusion of the capital. The library, the pretext for this academic foray, was in the middle of town, and my perusal of disintegrating books took place in a cacophony of hooting cars and yelling hawkers. This, however, was peace and quiet compared to the real heart of the city, the few blocks around the main Dessalines Avenue, where a market attracts an almost impenetrable mass of humanity.

It struck me then that people with no money spend an inordinate amount of time engaged in buying and selling. Vast piles of plastic bowls vied for attention with counterfeit watches; heaps of green bananas lay next to mountains of second-hand clothes shipped in from Miami. Even more cornucopian was the Iron Market, a stifling Victorian structure stuffed with paintings, religious artefacts and determined salesmen, from which I feared I'd never emerge.

Poverty in Port-au-Prince was sometimes shocking. Outside the cathedral, emaciated beggars seemed close to dying; mothers thrust babies at the few tourists; a sprawling slum area by the sea, La Saline, was an endless jumble of cardboard shacks and open sewers. But the city was also beautiful. Gaunt mountains, skeletal through deforestation, surrounded a perfect horseshoe bay. Eccentric filigree mansions half-hidden by bougainvillea stood on the hills. Elaborately decorated minibuses invoked divine protection, while lovingly hand-painted signs advertised restaurants and hairdressers. From high in the bourgeois suburb of Petionville, Port-au-Prince looked gorgeous, especially at night.

We hired a car and drove to the once-prosperous and nostalgia-ridden south coast port of Jacmel, full of crumbling gingerbread mansions. We visited the northern city of Cap-Haitien, the 'Paris of the Antilles' before the French were thrown out by the slave army. Here, in a scene Graham Greene might have relished, we met a Baptist coffin-manufacturer from the American Midwest who had come to do some good work. And, of course, we did what every visitor to Haiti should do: we marvelled at the Citadelle, the impregnable mountaintop fortress built by the mad King Christophe to withstand a French reinvasion that never happened.

Haitians were unfailingly kind and friendly, if sometimes a little hard to shake off when scenting dollars. The old cliché about dignity amid poverty came to mean something, as did the other one about creativity. Artists produced idyllic landscapes poignantly at odds with the dusty reality, sculptors fashioned mysterious icons out of recycled metal.

And Baby Doc, though he didn't know it, was living his last months of luxury in the gleaming white presidential palace. The following February, he was unceremoniously chucked out by his generals and the Americans. Things were supposed to get better, but they didn't. When I returned in 1987, the army was in charge, there were no tourists, violence was rising. I later heard that a politician had been shot dead in the hall of the Santos and that Madame had packed up and left for Florida.

It certainly made a change from France, and we returned uneaten. But something had bitten me; and I decided then that the academic life was not for me. Twenty years on, I'm still going to the Caribbean, though I'm afraid the varsity is no longer paying the air fare.

On 22 February 1985, sterling fell to its lowest ever level against the US dollar: a mid-price of $1.07, which meant some foreign exchange bureaux offered a rate of parity (£1 = $1).

MISSING FIDEL, 1985

Sara-Jane Hall tries to kick-start her radio career by interviewing *El Presidente*, but ends up on a Cuban chicken farm instead.

When your parents are committed socialists, holidays are different. There will be footpath-clearing holidays – wicked farmers being a constant threat to rights of way; there may be a self-improving element – historical, musical or artistic; or – in the name of internationalism – there may be town-twinning. There may even be somewhere exotic like Berlin, but only while its still behind the Iron Curtain. Mostly you go camping. These were my summertime memories as a child. I longed for Pontins and Lyme Regis the same way I longed for sliced white bread and Rice Krispies (banned at home).

Then something unlikely happened. After many years of bitter wrestling with tent frames and horror at hotel prices, Mum and Dad took themselves (but not me) off Somewhere Sunny. Somewhere hot. Somewhere with beach umbrellas, cocktails, scuba diving and lobster. Somewhere Caribbean in fact.

It was 1984 and my parents went on holiday to Cuba, coinciding neatly with the 25th anniversary of the Revolution. The New Socialist Caribbean Utopia of Cuba – so near to Florida and so unlike Moscow. This was an adventurous thing to do at the time. Our Party friends had braved Russia, coach tours of Poland, China, and even Welsh work camps. But Cuba? I was jealous. I considered myself the hardy traveller of the family, braving Egyptian borders and Ecuadorean slums. I even asked for an advance on my dowry to help fund a trip to the Middle East. I had become experienced at taking myself off as far as a student budget would let me go. But Cuba was something else.

Glancing over my parents' snapshots of rum-cocktail-strewn tables and exotic dancers I knew this was in another league of comfort, and adventure. So lush were their photos of cigar-rolling lovelies, their memories of salsa dancing, that I found it hard to equate these with their otherwise wholesome support of socialism. I knew I had to go.

It was 1985. I'd just joined the BBC as a trainee and was keen to 'get on'. So I headed off to the Cuban Embassy in London to see if I could make any contacts to do some recordings while I was there. After all, no one really knew much about Cuba outside of news reports on Fidel's speeches. I reckoned this could simultaneously get me an enviable suntan and kick-start my radio career. Cuba was undiscovered territory – pre-'Wallpaper' holiday suggestions, pre-just about everyone else discovering the joys of Caribbean Socialism (otherwise known as a beach holiday without the guilt). I proposed features on Hemingway, cigar factories, salsa, jazz et al. – remember these were not yet tired subjects – and made all my arrangements through the most radical of the 'Eastern bloc' travel companies.

So began a series of daily conversations with Landon Temple of Progressive Tours. As a student I had been used to organising every bit of the tour myself. In the Caribbean Socialist Utopia this was impossible. Everything had to be pre-booked and paid for, a near-impossible feat: the Cuban telephone system was antiquated, while telex served as a very primitive worldwide web. Mr Temple would always tell me that he was waiting for a telex from Havana, but that everything would be fine. And so it turned out – starting when I checked in for the Soviet Ilyushin routed from Moscow via Shannon in Ireland to Havana. The flight was unremarkable, apart from the aggression of the Aeroflot stewardesses, who hurled the in-flight meals at you with the sort of disgust that could only have come from having tasted the food already. The meal over, they had locked themselves in the hold (an unusual design feature of the jet made this feasible) to smoke, and refused to come out for the remainder of the flight.

As far as I could make out on arrival, I was pretty much the only Western visitor in the airport. I was five years too early for the first proper guidebook. US guides such *Fodor's Guide to the Caribbean* simply ignored the rebel island, so I didn't really know what to expect. Certainly not the faded grandeur of the Nacional Hotel. Sweeping up the drive in an imported Fiat taxi, led down endless corridors with the slanting light of louvered wooden doors that let too many smells and sounds from the rooms into the corridors, I was transported to a Humphrey Bogart film set. I never dreamed a few dollars a night could buy such luxurious surroundings. (It certainly can't these days, now that Cuba has embraced mass tourism as the economic saviour of the country.) My bedroom looked out over the sweep of Havana's Bay, the foreground lush with palm trees.

The luxury was only skin deep, though. Cockroaches crawled up my legs when I leaned against the lobby bar. The buffet epitomised monotony (chicken production must have been up, up, up that year). I was surrounded by the wives of the Soviet Communist cadres who had been given trips as rewards for devotion to duty in Moscow. They had shot-putt physiques and uniform green swimsuits. Yet there was still enough exotica to make me feel glamorous. I was treated like royalty by the staff – although this was due to the fact that I was probably the only hotel guest not to know of the existence of the no-tipping rule (again, long since revoked).

I was a touch disappointed to find two other journalists, from LBC and a Swedish national network, were already in residence. They were impressed by the appearance of the BBC, having no idea as to my extremely junior role in the Corporation. We swapped stories of bureaucratic difficulties: it had taken each of us a day of our lives to obtain an 'essential press identity card'; I lost mine immediately, and was never asked for it anyway. We agreed to stay in contact during our respective tours of the island. Influenced by my earlier incarnation as an intrepid backpacker, I had been overambitious in my Cuban travel plans. I had booked buses, hired cars, arranged hotel stays in distant towns, and struggled accordingly with a deeply undeveloped tourist system and an inflexible ration system. Three currencies confused matters: pesos, which we weren't supposed to have but which were on offer from black-marketeers everywhere; dollars, which we weren't meant to use anywhere but official government dollar shops; and a tourist currency akin to cigarette cards, which we were meant to use but no one wanted. I had driven down eight-lane motorways with no other cars in sight, except the odd broken-down Buick surrounded by crowds of passengers inspecting the engine. I found, without maps, pre-booked hotels empty except for rattling, churning fridges made in Minsk, and huge televisions showing scratchy reruns of military parades.

I arrived parched in the 'hero city' of Santiago de Cuba (so-called because this was where Fidel's revolutionary career began in 1953) to find no shops or cafés at which to buy water. Neat rum was the only drink freely on offer. The one location where this was not the case was the fast-developing Varadero beach resort, already warming up as the island's main tourist enclave, catering to charter-jet loads of French Canadians.

For three weeks, I lapped up all the idiosyncrasies of eastern-Europe-on-Sea. Finally, it was time to work. Things did not go well on the recording front. My press guide Eduardo filled my interview timetable with a near-steady stream of visits to those high-productivity chicken farms, tractor factories, hospitals and tobacco plantations. Eddie was late every day; an hour, an hour and a half . . . I cared less and less – one more interview in translation with a chicken farmer wasn't going to make this recording the career breakthrough I was hoping for.

'So, er, how many chickens do you have here?' Long translation session by Eddie, my state-provided fixer, with farmer. 'How is chicken production this year compared to last year?' Ditto. After three days and twelve tapes, the most usable item was a four-hour interview, entirely in Spanish, with the captain of Hemingway's fishing boat. I was almost relieved when, for two long days, I was trapped in the hotel by a hurricane. A day later I fell ill. That night, I hugged the toilet bowl for a twelve-hour stretch and awoke on the floor in the morning feeling extremely weak. The hotel doctor came and administered some vile pink medicine and then I slept. I woke, cried, and slept again.

Some 24 hours later, feeble and nauseous, I stumbled down to the lobby to see if Eddie had left a message. In my pigeonhole at the front desk I glimpsed a stack of new messages, but before I had time to wonder about my new-found popularity I was accosted by The Serious Swede and Mr·LBC Journalist, who had been staying in some distant wing of the hotel.

'Where the hell have you been?' Grunt of pain. Then, a most unexpected turn of events. 'We were meant to meet

Fidel Castro yesterday! *El Presidente*. Where the hell were you?' It seemed that, having heard of a coterie of Western journalists staying at the Nacional, someone had decided that an audience with Fidel might be to the leader's advantage. An interview had been approved at the highest level for myself and the others. An official driver had come to collect us from the Nacional but, finding 'the woman from the BBC' missing, had become suspicious and refused to take anyone at all to the meeting with Fidel. No matter how much pleading. 'Didn't you get a note? Didn't you hear us knocking, phoning?'

I had been too busy being either sedated or being sick. My complexion gave the truth of the story, so they stopped berating me. Holiday/career move at an end, I returned home to Britain paler and thinner than I'd hoped, and without meeting Fidel. Knowing I had come so close, but no closer, to meeting a living legend, left me feeling even sicker.

Five years passed before I visited Cuba again. This time, I was a little higher up the BBC ladder, and was making a series called *Sentimental Journey* for Radio 4 with writer and comedian Arthur Smith. The idea was that we took people back to significant places in their past. I came up with the idea of taking Arthur Scargill to Cuba – to relive his happy days as a regular recipient of Fidel's hospitality. The former miners' leader was an affable, easy and entertaining companion. Night after night he regaled us with tales of his dancing on the stage with the sequinned and G-string-wearing dancers at the Tropicana, and his wife's crush on Harry Belafonte, who was another of Fidel's personal guests along with the Scargills for the 25th anniversary celebrations (my parents missed out on that party). We drank daiquiris and mojitos, and I rediscovered the sensation of enjoying socialist decadence that my parents had first fallen upon. Forty years after the revolution, decadence had reached higher grounds, as 'ladies of the night', once banned in the new Cuba, appeared to have resurfaced with some force and pursued us through the streets of Havana calling out 'Eh! Arturo, Arturo!' Arthur Scargill reminisced and we listened and recorded.

He had been back to Cuba on more than one occasion and he told us of midnight assignations he had been invited to with Fidel Castro. It seemed that on every one of his previous visits the NUM President had received phone calls in his hotel room at the dead of night. He had been alerted and then whisked away to one of Fidel's secret hiding places, still being under constant threat of assassination, where the two revolutionary comrades would discuss world politics. Or rather Fidel would talk and Arthur would listen.

'He would talk for hours at a time,' Arthur confided. 'He speaks very good English actually. Just likes to pretend he can't to irritate the Americans. Loves to talk. In fact, I was out-talked by Fidel Castro,' he added, relishing the irony of this confidence. Scargill himself talked on and on. On occasions Arthur Smith would, in the face of such self-righteousness, cry in despair, 'Didn't you ever make a mistake? Don't you ever wake up and think "I was wrong about that"?' But to no avail. Arthur Scargill, in every situation it seemed, had been right.

From the start I had nudged him to make an approach to Castro, 'mentioning that we were in the vicinity and would love a chat'. No, I was reassured by Arthur, the all-seeing Fidel knew everything that was going on in his country and would definitely know he was there and would be 'in contact'. In a fever of anticipation – my audience with the living legend closer than ever – I woke every hour during the night. Every ding of the reception bell, every gurgle of the pipes aroused my suspicions. But once again it was not to be. Fidel the all-knowing, all-seeing, neither knew nor cared.

The nearest we got to a look at the inner workings of the Party was when I lost the programme tapes. On the final morning I woke early, showered and opened my backpack to listen back, with anticipated smugness, to what I believed were some of the best location recordings I had ever made – at the other end of the spectrum from monolingual chicken farmers. Scargill describing Che Guevara's waxwork, complete with genuine beret, in the former Presidential Palace, now the Museum of the Revolution; Scargill flirting with our guide Maria, a daughter of one of Fidel's inner circle; Scargill and Smith necking daiquiris while discussing the miners' unique contribution to the island's revolutionary history with a waiter in Hemingway's favourite bar.

But it was all gone. Not there. The recording machine, the tapes, everything. Where? I turned my room over and found no sign. Bedraggled and just showered I ran across the corridor to the still-sleeping Arthur Smith's room. My hysterical rantings roused him from his bed and he ran with me out of the hotel across to the restaurant of the night before. The indifferent, badly paid staff were different from the night before, knew nothing, said nothing, and we walked back despondently to our hotel. What could I do? Our flight was at noon. After this dream-like assignation I had nothing to show for it. We discussed the possible reactions to this catastrophe. My editor would be livid, would never forgive me, I said. 'Nah. He won't mind, he'll understand,' Arthur vainly reassured. 'Won't mind!' I screamed. 'I'll be dead meat!'

It was time to give the bad news to Arthur 2. By the time he opened his bedroom door I had been crying for an hour and experiencing stomach-ulcer-like symptoms. 'What is it!' he gasped, clutching my arm. 'Has someone died?' His thoughts had shot automatically to Yorkshire, and his family.

I explained the predicament and he was amazingly cool about the whole thing. After all, as he had just pointed out, no one had died. We sat on the terrace of the Hotel Inglaterra, overlooking the Parque Central in the heart of Havana, in despair. I suggested trying to redo the interviews and then adding sound effects afterwards. But as we started going over familiar ground ('So, Arthur, when did you first come to Cuba?'), we all knew the results would be a base element compared to the first take.

We had called Maria our guide – the daughter of the revolution, who had been so enamoured with Scargill's trade-union credentials – but she could offer no magic solution. Maria had disappeared without trace. With an hour to go before leaving for the airport, we sat despondently nursing bad coffees when a call came from reception. It was our guide and she had our tapes. Maria didn't (or couldn't) say how, but I had a sensation that coercion had taken place, and tapes found accordingly. I didn't care, I ran back to the previous night's restaurant and into the arms of my audio dynamite, dispensing dollar bills like confetti. Once again, I had failed to meet Fidel; but once again, I had definitely felt his touch.

In the summer of 1985, a Seattle-based adventure travel company called Society Expeditions announced plans for tourist space flights aboard the US space shuttle by 1992. The idea was suspended after the loss of the USS Challenger in January 1986.

THUMBING A LIFT INTO A FABULOUS LANDSCAPE, 1986

Hitchhiking around the Pacific Rim in 1986, Hamish Mykura entered the world of a Booker Prize novel.

Hitchhiking in New Zealand is an easy sport, and hitchhiking in a kilt there is really no sport at all. Like going fishing with dynamite in an aquarium, it's simply too easy.

I spent the summer of 1986 hitchhiking around the Pacific Rim, on the thin pretext of researching a graduate thesis on soil erosion. In Southeast Asia, my kilt was itchy and sweaty and regarded by drivers as some unfashionable variety of mini-sarong, and no one paid much attention to it at all. In California the man in the skirt by the roadside was assumed to be just another run-of-the-mill sex pervert. I'd reached the point where I was just about ready to sell the thing, and then I reached New Zealand.

Then I found what I'd been searching for – understanding, recognition, and really long lifts. I sped around the North Island in record time, and began the long southward haul down the eerie, alpine coast of the South Island.

At the end of the previous year, Keri Hulme's magic-realist Maori fable *The Bone People* had enraged the literary establishment by stealing the Booker Prize, and as the roads got narrower and the cars less frequent I had time to stand on the verge, book in one hand and thumb at the ready on the other, and read her strange evocations of the landscape around me.

Then I got stranded in the middle of nowhere: a long, long wait on flat, bleak farmland at the top of a windy hill down to the sea. The light was slowly being sucked out of the bedraggled scrubby sky, and there was a sudden spatter of big warm raindrops. I kept thinking of the peculiar bits in the book when Maori ancestors, powerful and malign, emerge alarmingly into reality.

A car rounded the corner, headlamps spotlighting the raindrops, and me. It passed, braked sharply, and came whining back. The door opened. 'Not many kilts on the Franz Josef road,' said a woman's voice. I got in, book on my lap, and we raced off. She had a big face and strong smile; something about the cheeks were slightly Maori.

She nodded at the book. '*The Bone People*?'

'Yes,' I said. 'Have you read it?'

'Actually,' she said, 'I wrote it.'

We looked at each other. *The Bone People* was fiction, but the person at the wheel was the sullen, brilliant heroine of the story.

We bounced along in the Hillman Avenger down a gravel road towards Okarito, population 21. Her town, tiny and inaccessible. 'It's off the beaten track: so not so many Germans.' That sounded good.

Between the wet gusts the moon would break through and show up a bare, slick landscape, punch-drunk from recent glaciation. I chattered about glaciers, pointing out moraines, U-shaped valleys, *roches moutonnées*. She seemed intrigued. 'How do you know about all this?'

Sheepish: 'I'm a geomorphologist.' Usually a conversation stopper. Clears parties in moments.

Wildly enthusiastic: 'Bloody hell! I always wanted to be a geomorphologist!' There was, I suppose, a kind of bonding. She asked me to come round that evening and I brought my plastic bottle of Johnny Walker, dead weight saved for a special occasion.

Her house was strange: hand-built and round, like a stubby lighthouse. I knew as I got near it that I was walking into the pages of the book. The beautiful octagonal tower room that is the centre of so much of the story's action was already completely familiar, and there it was, exactly as imagined, real to the last detail.

We drank and talked about glaciers and Maoris and the shape of New Zealand and the pages of the evening turned. The whisky was drunk and the conversation turned to racoons. Bloody pests in these parts, said Keri Hulme. Then we lifted down rifles from the medieval hooks on one wall of the room and stepped out into the night to shoot racoons.

In April 1986, the first weekend trip to Albania from Britain departed, price £195 for four days, travelling via Belgrade and Titograd (now Podgorica). A family of four on the tour was discovered to be smuggling in Bibles, but were allowed to cross the border back to Yugoslavia after the offending books were confiscated.

TECHNICOLOUR DREAM CÔTE, 1987

Fi Glover remembers a fortnight in the South of France with a blond, a camper van and a hostess dressed in Chanel.

Alex had natural rhythm. She could just get up on stage and dance. My dancing on the other hand made me appear to be having some kind of fit. But Alex persuaded seventeen-year-old me that it was a stunningly good idea to enter the Go Go Club's dance competition, held every Saturday at Juan Les Pins' finest nightspot. You had to get on stage and gyrate to Rick Astley for about two minutes. The person who made the crowd clap loudest won 50 francs, a sickly cocktail and the undying admiration of all the cocky French boys who wore their trousers too high and had packets of Dunhill wedged in their pockets. I am eternally grateful to the small contingent who applauded me in a desultory style out of sheer pity. I think Alex won the competition. I know that I came last.

It was the summer of 1987 and I had just finished my A-levels. I didn't really know Alex but we came from the same town in Hampshire and I had got bored with the people I was meant to be staying with in the South of France so I phoned her and, with the arrogance of that age, asked if I could come and stay at her infinitely plusher villa perched high on the hills above Cap d'Antibes.

A day later, I pitched up, as did two other Winchester stragglers. Jamie was tall and blond and sexy, and his friend was darker, duller but nevertheless appealing. He was called Jim or Tim or maybe even Dim. They had a VW combi that they had strapped together with bits of hope and spluttered down from Calais. I nearly wilted, I thought they were so cool. So me, Alex and her friend Kathy and Jamie and Dim spent two weeks haring round the corniche in a shabby van that smelled of boys and fags and booze. I thought life couldn't get any better.

I didn't realise that people actually lived in villas like Alex's, with manicured front gardens and pedicured back gardens overflowing bougainvillaea and the essential crystal-clear pool. Alex said that Ozzy Osborne had the villa next door, and we spent a lot of time peering over the incredibly high walls trying to catch of glimpse of a real rock star or at least a rock star's entourage. When we finally did see the occupants, they looked more like the kind of couple who came from a small town in Germany and went to swingers' parties at the weekends. But that didn't dull the allure of the Côte d'Azur. Ever since Coco Chanel turned the Cap d'Antibes into the melanoma Mecca of the Western world in the 1930s, it has attracted the kind of people who wear linen suits that don't crease and have skins to match their Louis Vuitton luggage.

Juan Les Pins sits in the bosom of the Côte, midway between Antibes and St Tropez. It's like a trashy white stiletto on an otherwise well-turned-out French woman. It's famous for two things: the jazz festival held there in May, and the fact that it's mentioned in the song 'Where do you go to, my lovely?' It's a pretty town that is now slightly dwarfed by the big blocks of flats on the seafront. The population is small in winter but swells to unbearable proportions every summer when Europe's moneyed elite descend and sit around the cafés on the promenade making sure they look as rich as everyone else. With Cannes, Nice and the Principality of Monaco all within shouting distance it's a magnet for the kind of ladies who always have their bikini lines waxed.

Their blokes are invariably older and have white gin palaces that they moor in the tiny harbour at Juan. The villas up on Cap d'Antibes once hosted parties for the likes of the Fitzgeralds and then for Brigitte Bardot. Now Joan Collins and George Michael have taken over.

Nobody seems to do very much apart from tan and chat in Juan Les Pins. But for those two weeks in 1987 it didn't matter. We didn't have many plans anyway apart from working out which direction to send our hopping hormones in – so we just cruised around and sniggered at the smart people on the pay beaches. The boys had ridiculously small trunks on and seemed genuinely concerned about tanning their buttocks to the max . . . and the girls had the kind of upwardly nubile boobs that even after childbirth probably won't look like two fried eggs sliding out of opposite sides of a frying pan.

I was amazed at the fact that people paid to go on beaches just because some poor geezer came along and raked the sand in front of their loungers every hour on the hour. We spent most of our days on the public beaches that are far more suited to the kind of throwing and kicking games that you always end up playing when you see some sand.

Most of all, though, I was awed into silence by Alex's mum who was the epitome of elegance. She wore about seven outfits during the course of the day. She had a swimming outfit, a lunch outfit and when she drove into Juan to buy dinner in the afternoon she changed into a Chanel suit. Her kind of shopping seemed to consist of buying two baguettes, a fat bunch of parsley and some French beans. With this minimal load she'd go into the kitchen and turn it all into a salade nicoise for the five new house guests that had suddenly descended on her calm. I'd never met anyone like her. She used to tell Alex which clothes went with which hairstyle, a conversation that my mother had never felt the need to have with me. She put up with us spluttering home in the combi at ungodly hours of the morning, and skinny dipping and doing nonsense things just because it was the middle of the night – and when we ran out of tabs she kindly allowed us to bum long, thin Peter Stuyvesant cigarettes off her.

My eyes hurt by the end of our trip because I'd stared at people so much. I think I promised myself that one day I'd be that elegant and have lots of outfits and do things with parsley and beans. In fact my sister and I made a drunken pact one night after I got back from the Côte d'Azur experience. We said that when we were 60 we'd live in a big villa on Cap d'Antibes and wear lopsided bouffant wigs and dodgy full make-up and tan ourselves to the point of leather. Thankfully neither of us still hold that ambition close to our hearts.

The last I heard of Alex she was doing something dangerously close to lap dancing in a nightclub – perhaps she was inspired by her win at the Go Go club. I bumped into Jamie once a couple of years ago: he was flogging photocopiers in Fulham Broadway. I don't know what happened to Jim, or Tim or Dim. The combi van collapsed on its way back to Britain and is probably still in a lay-by off the autoroute.

I went back to Juan Les Pins recently as part of a new job. I'd forgotten about the dreadful dancing competition – until I turned on the radio while we were speeding east up the corniche late at night. An Americanised DJ came on the dial playing one of those self-congratulatory jingles that are meant to make you think that you're listening to the station that has interviewed all the stars. 'Hi! I'm George Michael', 'Hi! I'm Barry White', 'Hi! I'm Rick Astley'. I think I had the grace to blush in the car.

On 30 January 1987, the government's shares in British Airways went on sale. Six months later, BA took over its nearest rival, British Caledonian.

SILENT AND SLUMBERING, 1987

The veil between gods and mortals was drawn back for
Jessica Morris on a hot Sicilian sojourn.

During the last tutorial of term a compulsory month at an
Italian language school was announced. I recoiled in horror
at delighted shrieks of 'let's share a flat in Florence!' I wanted
something magical to happen, not a sleep-over. And then an
afterthought from Dr McLaughlin: 'Don't suppose any of you
fancy a place in Sicily called Erice?'

I was reading Italian as a result of my bookish teens, and
an overactive yearning for high romance. I knew little of
modern Italy, even less about Sicily. The points of reference
I armed myself with were at least two thousand years old –
that the Cyclops had lived in the area; that Erice had once
been the centre of the cult of Venus; and that it was named
after her son, Eryx. Other than that I had seen *The Godfather*
and expected to spend my summer surrounded by women
with headscarves and toothless men riding donkeys.

I fantasised about arriving in Palermo harbour by steamer,
but practicality – and the overnight train – prevailed. I didn't
feel too hard done by; my fellow couchette travellers
included a very small and ancient couple in their black
Sunday best, who crossed themselves whenever the train
pulled out of a station, a soldier with melting chocolate eyes
on leave from National Service, and a poet who gave me a
signed copy of his latest collection of verse.

At dawn we reached Scilla. The train uncoupled and
shunted on to the ferry to cross the straits of Messina. On
deck I watched the coast of the mainland disappear, while a

strange, discordant music filled the brisk morning air. I knew it was only heated train wheels cooling, but to me it was the siren's song and I braced myself to see the clashing rocks of Charybdis close in on us.

Palermo: chaos, children hawking pirate tapes from handcarts, my bus to Trapani nowhere to be found. Anxious, hot, unable to make myself understood in Italian. And then my first experience of the kindness of strangers in the Mezzogiorno: a passer-by walked me to the 'bus stop' (a stretch of main road with nothing to distinguish it from its surroundings) and fed me my first *arancino*, a deep-fried ball of rice with a spicy meat sauce at its heart, the essential initiation rite for the foreigner in Sicily, the taste of home for the Sicilian in exile. One last connection in Trapani and I was alone on a bus roaring its vertiginous way up the side of a sheer cliff, the driver sounding a deafening klaxon at intervals but seemingly oblivious to the precipice that swung towards me as we rounded the hairpin bends. We pulled into a deserted car park near the top of the mountain. In the pidgin adopted by all native speakers when addressing foreigners, the driver flapped at me: 'Here! Erice! Off!'

Mid-afternoon in the Mediterranean, and nothing stirred. Before me a parapet and vast blue view across the haze of Trapani, sea on either side, to the Egadi islands floating on the horizon. Behind, an ancient stone wall. I panted and slipped my way up polished cobbles in the welcome shade of flanking blind walls, which gave no hint of the elaborate courtyards within. Everything was silent and slumbering and the bubble of anxiety in my stomach started to turn to anticipation. I passed under an alcoved bridge, with its protecting Madonna lit up in electric blue. A sharp bend to the left and the piazza opened up before me. Shuttered shops, utter stillness. I could feel the atmosphere, as thick with concentrated quiet as a church. And then a voice from nowhere said, '*Ciao*, Jessica!'

My first thought, before reason returned, was that Virgil knew his stuff – there *are* moments when the veil separating gods and mortals is drawn back. Eryx had welcomed me.

I still resist the subsequent explanation that a girl from my tutorial group, arriving early, had found herself a boyfriend (today her husband), and he knew I'd be on the afternoon bus. I remember nothing of the classes we took. But I can walk every step of that first evening as I headed for the piazza, when a great curl of smoke came tumbling down the roof and wall of the building in front of me, followed by another and another on all sides so that I stopped in concern, and a woman leaning out of a high window called down to me, her voice cracking with laughter, '*E' la nebbia!*' (It's the fog!) Although I didn't understand her, she sounded so happy about it I carried on reassured.

To start with, each evening we would gather in the piazza outside Bar Nzino while the *passeggiata*, the evening parade of finery, passed by the watery gaze of a dozen old men sitting on plastic chairs outside their social club. Then we wandered to the Balio, scrubby formal gardens that over looked the site of Venus's temple, now a ruined Norman fortress. There we sat, listless in the heat, and listened to Piero the architecture student play Italian love songs on his guitar, while my curly-blonde roommate showed off by knowing all the words.

Away from Curly Blonde I felt more at my ease. I met Salvatore, more commonly known by one of those nicknames the Italians always use as a sign of ironic respect, in his case *Il Ragoniere* (the Accountant), who told me folk tales of 'Cola Pesce, who swam like a fish and sacrificed himself far beneath the sea to hold up a cracked pillar keeping Sicily afloat'. I spent an evening being trounced at dominoes by Bruno, the dark angel with a duelling scar who was determined to go straight, but was still hailed by cries of '*Barone!*' when he walked into the bar. I was lionised briefly by shifty Guido, home for the summer to show off a Maserati he had somehow bought on the proceeds of a fish restaurant in Bologna. I spent an afternoon on the beach with his beautiful, guileless kid brother Aldo, who years later I heard died of an overdose while trafficking, which finally explained the Maserati.

One evening, up at the Balio while Curly Blonde was flirting fluently with the boy she knew I liked, I was hit by a sudden revelation. My first act of true independence was formed; I didn't enjoy her company, and it was up to me to stay or go. I slipped away from the back of the *compania*, the circle of friends, and headed back towards the bar where I knew I would be welcome. Under the blue Madonna some sixth sense made me turn back and peer through the fog. In the diffused light of a street lamp Piero was hurrying after me. We sat talking in a back room of the bar until the tables were stacked with chairs and they gave us the key to lock up.

Piero took me to a free concert by an Italian rock legend in the main square of Palermo, a summer tradition all over the country. As Lucio Dalla sang his signature bittersweet anthem, around us everyone held up their lighters and swayed, and it didn't feel contrived. After the crowds had gone off to find ice creams the streets were littered with soft-drink cans, not a bottle of beer in sight.

Piero led me round the family-run restaurants of Trapani, feeding me on fish couscous and paper-thin pizza served crisp from the oven on to a tablecloth of greaseproof paper. Once, he refused to tell me what was in store, and drove me way along the coast towards Palermo, to a *pasticceria* where they made a wonderful tiramisu. He showed me the Erice he saw, a palimpsest of cultures left by centuries of conquering powers. As we stood leaning our palms against stone hewn by Carthaginians to build the town walls, he told me in confidence that his family had lost everything during the war.

'Who took it?' I asked, scandalised.

'*I Borboni*. The Bourbons,' he replied solemnly.

On my last day the fog lay thicker than ever on the ground. Piero took me to the altar of Venus to make a wish. He said that when the fog appears in Erice it means Venus is reaching out her arms to protect true lovers.

If Hollywood scriptwriters are to be believed, each of us should have a long, golden summer during which we learn to do the lambada, have a defining moment and fall in love for the first time. So maybe my Sicilian summer was a cliché. I didn't learn the lambada, but I did start to learn Italian. My defining moment came when I decided to walk away from Curly Blonde's little game. And I did fall in love under the blue Madonna, twice. Even if one of those loves is now lost, my love for Sicily will always be with me.

Shortly after leaving Zeebrugge, destination Dover, *Herald of Free Enterprise* capsized with the loss of 187 lives.

THE CITY IN SEARCH OF A SOUL, 1988

The BBC's sports correspondent at Seoul, Frank Partridge, recalls the last time the Olympics visited the Pacific Rim.

Seoul was a surprising choice as the host city of the 1988 Olympiad, but in the event, a sensible one. South Korea's Games signalled the revival of the Olympic movement, which was on its knees after a twenty-year battering from international politics. The country may have had virtually no Olympic pedigree, but, more importantly, it had few political enemies (apart from the Big One, lurking less than thirty miles away across the Demilitarised Zone).

It is easy to forget that Los Angeles had no rivals for the 1984 Games. Nobody else wanted them. And although the US created a TV spectacular with profits to match, it was by no means a global event – the Soviet Union, East Germany, and Cuba all boycotted it. This was payback time for Moscow 1980, when the Americans had snubbed 'the evil empire'.

But Seoul was almost boycott-free. Cuba (as usual) and North Korea (naturally) stayed away, but just about every Olympic gold medal was worthy of the title. The problem was filling the stadiums. The locals turned up whenever South Korea had a chance of a medal, but otherwise were scarcely to be seen. For the rest of the world, the expense and inconvenience of travelling to a country still a long way off the tourist trail was too daunting.

So the South Koreans duly built a velodrome, baseball stadium, rowing regatta centre and a (particularly fine) tennis arena. They were half full during the Games and, you couldn't help feeling, would be totally neglected after the

Olympic circus moved on. I'd love to find out what happened to all those lavish constructions Mr Samaranch instructed them to build.

Korea was such an unknown destination that the British Olympic team opted to train in Japan. British Airways started flying from Heathrow to Seoul just before the Games, but has since abandoned the route. Few visitors see the fruits of the breathless rebuilding programme that took place in the seven years between winning the Games and staging them.

Thirty-five years after the end of the Korean War, I was told by a local that the city centre contained only one pre-war building. Another story, possibly apocryphal, was that the main motorway into town could be converted within minutes into a runway for fighter jets in case of invasion from the north. There was a giant population scoreboard in the city centre that clicked up every few seconds to denote the birth of a new baby. There were monumental new hotels everywhere.

What the planners couldn't inject into Seoul was some soul. New squares and piazzas were gaudily decorated in Olympic regalia, but always lacked a crowd. Perhaps ordinary folk had been bussed out – a frequent fate for indigenous peoples when the Olympics come to town. I saw Arnold Schwarzenegger stroll around Seoul's city centre unrecognised and unmolested.

Even the magnificent and architecturally ground-breaking National Stadium itself, for the most part, had surplus capacity. Around the arena in the tense minutes before the Ben Johnson–Carl Lewis 100 metres showdown, I counted row upon row of empty seats. An American athlete said it felt like 'just another small-town meet'.

Ah yes, Ben Johnson. Seoul's other misfortune was that no matter how many nations came to the party, the 1988 Olympiad would go down in history as the 'Ben Johnson

Games'. Athletics lovers had endured a decade or more of East Europeans of unlikely physique carrying off cartloads of medals that everyone knew – but couldn't prove at the time – were ill-gotten. History has confirmed all suspicions. But Ben Johnson was different. At Seoul, a global superstar was caught red-handed as a user of performance-enhancing drugs and stripped of the Olympics' most coveted medal: and within days, not years, of winning it.

The men's 100 metres was a 'big story' whatever happened: Johnson, the glowering world-record holder; Lewis, the hero of the 1984 Games. For the final, I was right behind BBC Radio commentator Ian Darke. It all happened so quickly. I can clearly remember Darke's words: 'Johnson's got Lewis in his pocket . . .' as the Canadian pulled away, arms pummelling like a boxer's as he pushed the air aside. Linford Christie was third across the line.

Olympic finals rarely produce world records and the pundits had been predicting 10.02. But now there appeared a sequence of digits that took almost as long as the race itself to take in: 9.79. I was carried away with the significance of what I'd seen. Or thought I'd seen. I took a deep breath, wrote my 'Canadian Underdog Tames Uncle Sam' story, and recited the words down the line to London.

Two days later, at around 4.30 a.m. local time, the phone rang in my hotel room. I recognised the voice of the duty news editor. While I groped for the bedside light, I remember thinking that there had better be a good reason to wake me up at this hour. There was.

In 1988, the BBC team travelled to Korea on Cathay Pacific via Dubai, Hong Kong and Taipei, a total journey of 23 hours. The present nonstop journey on Korean Air takes half as long.

TIANANMEN – STILL HARD TO FORGET, 1989

Two years after the massacre, Tom Kelly revisited the square – and, beyond the ice-cream vendors, it was obvious the Party had rewritten history.

Could it really be the same place? I recalled the television images – mangled bikes, crushed tents, bloody corpses being carried away on rickshaws. A lone protester defying a line of tanks. Six weeks of heady heroism followed by the shock of the violent denouement – a horror movie brought into homes around the world on the small screen.

On 4 June 1989 I was teaching in southwest China when the troops moved into Tiananmen Square. I still recall hearing the news on the BBC World Service over a Sunday morning breakfast. I knew at once that life in China would never be the same again. And when I finally left – two summers later – the last thing I did was to revisit Tiananmen Square. It had seen history before. On 1 October 1949, Chairman Mao stood on the balcony of the Forbidden City and declared that the Chinese people had stood up. Communism had arrived, and with it the promise of a new society. In 1966 he stood there again, this time to launch the Great Proletarian Cultural Revolution. A million adoring Red Guards filled the 100-acre square, waving their Little Red Books as they chanted the name of their god.

The Cultural Revolution had turned sour and was now described as the 'Ten Lost Years'. Mao had been officially declared '70 per cent good'. And Tiananmen Square had witnessed its greatest drama yet. According to the *People's*

Daily, it had been the scene of 'a great victory'. Everyone else called it a massacre.

But was it true? The Chinese would have us believe that it never happened, that the horror movie on our screens was a product of Western fiction. They could rewrite, even eradicate, history for a grateful population only too glad to remove the guilt from their collective consciousness. They could turn the square back from a symbol of repression into one of prosperity at the heart of a modern city, so visitors to Tiananmen would think about the future, not the past.

And they had done it. When I returned, there was no trace of 1989. Children flew kites around the Monument to the People's Heroes, which two years earlier had been the rebel headquarters. Pedlars sold Mickey Mouse masks and candied hawthorns on sticks. Lovers posed for photographs in front of Chairman Mao's portrait and ice-cream vendors did business under enormous parasols. Sleek black limos cruised the boulevards around the square but, on Tiananmen itself, all traffic was forbidden.

The square belonged to the people. The atmosphere was more street party than Communist Party. To the north was the Forbidden City, where generations of emperors led sheltered lives in palaces of ivory and jade. Next door, behind a high wall, the new emperors took refuge from their subjects in the new forbidden city, the party and state compound of Zhongnanhai.

To the west was the Great Hall of the People, built by volunteer labour in 1959 at the height of the Great Leap Forward, when China aimed to overtake Britain's economy in fifteen years and the people really believed it could be done. These days the Great Hall houses the Congress chamber where China's parliament meets each spring for its two-week annual charade of democracy. I joined a guided tour and watched the Chinese day-trippers amuse themselves by sitting in the deputies' chairs and toying with the electronic voting devices.

To the east was the Museum of the Revolution, constantly being adapted to take account of each new shift in the political wind. A photograph of student protesters in 1919, astonishingly dated 4 June, was captioned: 'Patriotic students calling for democracy.' Hadn't anyone noticed the irony? Then there was a 'primitive wooden ploughshare' designed to illustrate the suffering of peasants under feudalism. In Guizhou, where I had been teaching, the farmers still used those in the fields.

To the south, a dutiful queue of pilgrims filed slowly across the square, passing the sculptures of model workers, soldiers and peasants on their way into the chairman's mausoleum. The men removed their caps as they walked silently past the crystal sarcophagus, then joined the queue at the souvenir stall to buy cigarette packets bearing Mao's name. Fifty yards away, the world's largest Kentucky Fried Chicken was churning out chicken and chips to Chinese youths anxious to demonstrate their support for Western values. A meal costs several days wages, but there was no shortage of takers.

The chairman looked down sternly from half a mile away across the square, those large brown eyes surveying a scene that he had been determined to resist. Capitalism, fashion, fast food and tourism had taken over where once there was revolutionary purity and hysteria. A great victory – or a massacre?

On 2 May 1989, Hungarian border troops begin to dismantle their stretch of the 'Iron Curtain' frontier with Austria. The move triggered mass emigration from East Germany and the collapse of Eastern European communism. The same week, the *Travellers' Survival Kit: Soviet Union and Eastern Europe* was published.

IN SEARCH OF THE PERFECT HOLIDAY – AND A TV, 1989

The Massif Central – Sharon Gethings remembers steep hills, magnificent views, wild flowers, the best croissant ever and a hapless, football-mad boyfriend.

May 1989 reminds me of aching calves, beautiful French countryside – and the Everton and Liverpool FA Cup Final. My boyfriend and I were visiting France together for the first time, and we had opted for one of those cushy cycling tours where your luggage is carried from location to location by the travel company. My main prerequisite was a bike with more than one gear – I had spotted those close-knit contour lines on the map in our travel kit; my boyfriend, a lifelong Reds fan, merely desired a radio or television on the day of the big match.

The starting point of our four-day journey was Aurillac, a small town at the southwest of the Parc Regional des Volcans, an area on the Massif Central where volcanic activity has created an undulating landscape perfect for hikers and cyclists. As we pedalled out of the town, the early summer weather was glorious and we had the road to ourselves.

The silence intensified the impact of the scenery as it gradually unravelled: gentle inclines gave way to fully fledged hills. The bucolic idyll was shattered at the bottom of a particularly steep section when a guard dog – unleashed, mark you – decided to fulfil his job description and violently chase me. I can only thank the misplaced mutt for another milestone of that summer: it is the only time I have cycled up a hill faster than I have freewheeled down the other side.

For every minor hiccup like this, though, nature seemed to offer compensation. One day, after struggling up the Everest of the hills on our route, cursing my lack of fitness, I discovered that a broken brake block had been pressing on my back tyre during the ascent.

Red-faced and cursing, I turned the final corner to berate my boyfriend for not waiting, only to have the words evaporate in gasps of awe when I saw the view. Thousands of feet below us a glinting silver thread wound through a billowing carpet of foliage that seemingly contained every shade of green possible. Here and there, a sprinkling of yellow signalled an acre or so of jonquil flowers or gentians, and high above this, clinging to the steep side of the valley, there was what looked like a doll's house, bolstered in its perch by timber stilts.

On another occasion, my boyfriend came off his bike and punctured a tyre attempting to avoid a snake sprawled across the road. The midday heat was intense and we were not looking forward to a long walk along more of the same dusty and unshaded road we had been climbing for the past hour. But a gentle curve in the road revealed a dip down to a cool riverside path, shaded beneath fat-leaved trees. It was almost as if someone was unravelling an ever-changing and ever-suitable landscape around us.

Exhilarated by each day's events we would wheel into the village where we were to spend the night, find our hotel and look for a bar with a television. Unfortunately, the destinations our itinerary took in seemed football-phobic; my heart bled for my boyfriend as Auvergnat after smiling Auvergnat employed the Gallic shrug to shatter his hopes of a glimpse of the game.

His plight was eased by the delights of our lodgings: an outwardly unpromising one-star *pension* offered up cool linen sheets on an antique bed and the best croissants ever in the morning; a farmhouse we reached at the end of a particularly gruelling day had – oh joy! – an outdoor hot tub; a half-timbered hotel in a pretty medieval town had a candle-lit restaurant where we dined to the sound of centuries-old church bells.

Sometimes it's only possible to appreciate perfection in retrospect, and I doubt that it's possible to plan it. I had faced the steepest hill of our trip practically with my brakes locked on and my boyfriend never did get to see the match, but, yes, I would say now that this was a perfect holiday (oh, and Liverpool won the final).

The bargain of the summer in July 1989 was a two-day trip from Gatwick to Istanbul, including accommodation, for £109.

THE CALM BEFORE THE DESERT STORM, 1989

Muthena Paul Alkazraji visited Baghdad before the first Gulf War and found a thriving city heavy on politics.

My entry into Iraqi airspace in the summer of 1989 began with an indignity in an airborne convenience. At 40,000 feet above the mountains of Kurdistan, as I occupied a WC on an Iraqi Airways 747, a fellow passenger tried to force an entry. It was an understandable error. The door's lock was broken and I had been holding it to with my feet. He pushed, and I pushed back.

He then pushed back harder. I held off the assault for about 30 seconds until I snarled: 'Do you mind!' He barked something back in Arabic and retreated.

I was flying to Baghdad during a brief respite in Iraq's perennial tribulations to visit my father. The war with Iran was over; the Allies had not yet assembled their military hardware among the Bedouin sands for the liberation of Kuwait. Nor had much of Iraq's infrastructure been shelled to rubble.

As we stepped off the plane at Baghdad the heat pushed us in the face like a hot air vent on maximum. We were bused to the terminal building beneath large neon lettering that spelled out unambiguously: Saddam International Airport. We filed past shifty security personnel wearing mirror-lens sunglasses and casually tonguing government-issue toothpicks, before entering baggage reclaim. It was here that two men I had never met before greeted me like the returning prodigal son, embracing and kissing me on each cheek. I took it as the customary Arabic greeting.

My father greeted me too, a little less demonstratively. (That evening when I was introduced at a dinner party, I heartily embraced the first person presented. 'No,' he scoffed stiffly. 'Too familiar.' I sheepishly shook the remaining guests' hands.)

Outside the airport we climbed into a Chevrolet and the two men, who turned out to be ingratiating junior employees at my father's office, drove us swiftly into the heart of the city. I sat in the back like a diplomat.

I stayed with my father for the next four weeks, in a suburb close to the city's football stadium. When I was killing time at his house, an entertainment highlight would be the regular broadcasts of Iraqi TV news. The theme music built up to a dramatic intensity fit for any Hitchcock climax, but the domestic coverage that followed was little more than scenes of government officials wandering serenely around hotel foyers to the strains of Vivaldi.

When my father was not tied to his desk, we drove around Baghdad in air-conditioned comfort, visiting the city's sites and souks. He bought me a pair of 'proper trousers' (brown acrylic, with a crease down the front). 'Do you want me to grow a moustache like Freddy Mercury's? Then I will be a complete Arab,' I said. We stopped at open-air restaurants for chickpeas, shish kebabs and Shahrazad beers, and dropped in on relatives and friends who fed us with okra and rice, wedges of watermelon and tiny glasses of sweet tea. His friends were invariably delighted to meet someone from England; so many of them had studied in the UK.

We drove past the ugly Unknown Soldier's Monument in Zawra Park, with its two giant arms clasping sabres to form an arch. Helmets of Iranian soldiers had been tastefully hung at the base.

We visited the towering split dome of the Martyr's Monument; my father had been personnel manager for

Brazilian labour brought in to build it. His days working there had, he said, been good times. On one occasion he had mistakenly driven up a road towards a presidential compound. Worse, his old van had backfired, alarming and severely irritating the Republican Guard. He was imprisoned for fourteen days for this. To relieve his boredom, the Brazilians performed samba music below his cell windows.

On another occasion some Brazilians had decided it would be amusing to draw a giant pair of spectacles on a public painting of Saddam Hussein. They were all thrown in jail, and my father managed to return their favour by securing their release.

We also cruised past the intriguing Ali Baba's Monument, where a statue of Murjana pours boiling oil on to the heads of the 40 thieves hiding in pots below. I spent a further day immersed in the Assyrian and Babylonian archaeology at the Iraq Museum, and we browsed around the copper and carpet merchants off Rashid Street. Baghdad was buzzing and prospering. At many sites I caused my father anguish by taking photographs too close to government buildings, or with soldiers in the frame (easily done in Baghdad). More than once he pulled over for a shot of gin to calm his nerves.

One evening we ate by the banks of the Tigris at a fish restaurant on Abu Nuas street. Here the fat Mazgouf fish were kept in tanks and pegged out around tamarisk wood fires to grill. Here, with the palm trees rustling, my father dozed and broke wind like a satisfied caliph.

In the bar of the Al-Rashid hotel – where the Western media set up camp two years later during the Gulf conflict, and from where CNN beamed out pictures of missiles steering their ominous course over the suburbs – we got chatting to a group of English businessmen. At the time I guessed they might be a party of refrigerator salesmen from

Wetherby; history now offers a few alternatives. 'Did you know,' I proclaimed boldly, 'that Amnesty International has documented grave human rights violations here?' It was a bit of a conversation-stopper; panic flashed across my father's face. Back at the car I was severely ticked off.

My final week in Baghdad was none too relaxing. Between the airline office and home my ticket vanished, and they would not reissue me with another booking until four days after my visa expired. This meant getting a visa extension. Every day we would return to the immigration office on Sa'doun Street to collect my passport, and the officials would grin and tell us to come back next day. My father told me not to look so stressed; it might make them suspicious. This made me more stressed and aroused their suspicions. They handed the passport over eventually, and I flew home.

My father remained in Baghdad throughout the Allied air raids in January and February 1991. He told me later how he sat on the roof of a bomb-shelter and watched anti-aircraft guns rake the sky like fireworks. There, at least, he figured he could see when a missile was heading towards him.

I have not been back to Baghdad since, but if stability ever comes to the country, I hope to.

In the summer of 1989, airlines from America offered the best-value tickets within Europe; to fly between London and Berlin, the cheapest fares were with Pan Am and TWA, both now defunct.

1990s and beyond

MELTDOWN IN ARGENTINA, 1990

In the southern summer of 1990, Sophie Campbell hitched her way from Buenos Aires to Patagonia – with heat spiralling as fast as inflation.

January 1990: Batman fever is sweeping Argentina. All my young cousins – down at Mar del Plata for their summer holidays – are wearing 'Bati' beach shoes and 'Bati' bermudas. The austral is 4,000 to the dollar and rising. Girls on the beach are wearing frills and G-strings and the football selectors in Buenos Aires are mulling over the World Cup squad that will later stun them by losing to Cameroon.

I sit in a brothel in Bahia Blanca, waiting for Monique. At this stage I don't know it is a brothel and I don't know if she will turn up. We have met just once, through our relatives, and the only thing we have in common is that we want to hitchhike around Argentina.

She arrives at 6 p.m., with a sleeping bag in one hand and a red leather hatbox in the other. Her equipment for the year is: two pairs of shorts, two T-shirts, jeans, jumper, hiking boots, sketch book, pictures of her home in Ireland and nail scissors for cutting her hair. We end up in our sleeping bags in the same bed, all the others being in hectic use by this time of night.

Bahia Blanca is a port and a good place to pick up trucks on the long run south to Patagonia. Being female is an immeasurable advantage. The drivers are carrying cash to pay for their petrol and robberies are on the increase. In courtly Argentina women are considered incapable of such a thing, so we sail past male students who may have to wait days for a lift. The longer the beard, the longer the wait. One Falklands veteran has been waiting for ten days; the pump attendants refer to him as 'el loco Malvino' and take him sandwiches when they can.

The truckers confound our every expectation. They eat very little, for fear of putting on weight or dozing off. They are intensely domesticated, pouncing on stray biscuit crumbs in their cabs and falling prey to the cleaning-product salesmen who lurk at service stations. They have a macho swagger, hitting the tyres with baseball bats to check their condition and cutting up their food with their *facons* (the knife that every red-blooded male carries at his belt). And yet their patron saint is La Difunta Correa, who died with her baby at her breast but continued to suckle it until it was found. Sentiment and hardship go hand in hand in this job. Doubly so during an economic meltdown.

Ruta 3 is the road that follows the edge of the Atlantic all the way down to Tierra del Fuego. It is a strip of grey flanked by dirt shoulders big enough to accommodate two trucks side by side, rippling into a heat haze on the horizon. We climb into cab after cab, sometimes with one driver, sometimes with two.

Monique and I seem to represent a third sex to the drivers. At our age, 28, most Argentine women are married with children and not climbing into trucks with strange men. Yet we do not fit into the category of the road prostitutes who ply their trade back and forth between service stations. So our offers of food are waved away, lifts are procured, solicitous questions are asked. Monique, who has very little money, touches a chord. But there is more; a peculiar generosity born of crisis which we meet everywhere. In the heat and the desperation and the spiralling inflation, people stick together.

As the austral creeps past 5,000 to the dollar and rumours of President Menem's marital problems begin to filter south, we are still going nowhere in particular. Where the trucks go, we go: Welsh Patagonia, with its permanent moaning wind and thorn bushes festooned with plastic bags; the snaggletoothed mountains of Tierra del Fuego; the glaciers of Lago Argentino. Our Spanish, now laced with *lumfardo* – the Argentine equivalent of rhyming slang – is coming on in leaps and bounds and will deeply shock my Buenos Aires cousins at a later date. We drink quantities of *mate*, a herb tea which suppresses your appetite, turns your tongue green and signals a halt for conversation.

There are other advantages. In undulating country like this, there is no better way to see than from the cab of a flat-front truck. High above fence level, with a panorama of rabbit-fur colours and infinite blue skies scrolling past in the windscreen, the drivers point out guanacos, armadillos, Patagonian hares. They tell us incredible stories of an estancia of mythical proportions owned by the Queen, and that the biggest landowner on the Malvinas is none other than devil incarnate herself, La Thatcher. I have started to read *One Hundred Years of Solitude*, the bible of South American magic realism. But as the austral romps into the high six thousands, and the price of a meal goes up as I am eating it in a roadside café, it just seems like realism to me.

In the summer of 1990, England lost a penalty shoot-out against Germany in the semi-final of the World Cup; the Germans went on to beat Argentina in the final.

BOWLED OVER BY BOSTON, 1990

New England was just a stepping stone between California and England. But it was also a kind of coming home for Lucy Gillmore.

In 1990, I was looking for 'old' America – Henry James, white clapboard houses, picket fences and steepled churches. I had just spent a year at the University of California, Berkeley, as part of an exchange programme with St Andrews in Scotland, and had decided to stop off on the way home to visit my friend Elizabeth on Cape Cod.

Taking classes with titles like Women and Silence (an unsurprisingly vocal and totally female course) and Shakespeare and Film (the Bard in Technicolor for surfers and frat boys) and lodging with an erratic divorced psychiatrist, her disturbed daughter and their enormous, slobbering St Bernard, Hildie, had left me in a state of irreversible culture shock. I'd survived a major earthquake and fraternity parties and was suffering from daytime soap addiction.

Reeling from a last-ditch tie-dye assault in Berkeley's hippie haven, Telegraph Avenue, the names Sandwich, Barnstable, Yarmouth and Falmouth conjured up images of sleepy coastal villages and lured me away to the Cape. I felt that I needed to escape to a place where the answer 'England' didn't automatically meet with the question: 'New England?'

Elizabeth had studied in St Andrews for a year and was now a reporter for Cape Cod Newspapers in East Yarmouth. Her apartment was over a shop, optimistically named Antiques of the Future, in the tiny village of Cotuit. A traditional New England building painted pale grey and white and surrounded by trees, it had a separate entrance up a wooden staircase at the side, leading on to a sunny deck.

While Elizabeth was at work I pottered around the flat with Corretta, her schizophrenic cat, or wandered along the lane to the beach. The good hour it took to walk, shaded by overhanging trees, and passing overgrown hedgerows and the large clapboard holiday homes of wealthy Bostonians, fed my Henry James fantasy.

Stopping off at the grocery store, I would buy ice cream and listen lethargically to local gossip before continuing on to the beach – small, golden and fringed by swaying grasses and smooth dunes. The water was clear and cool, and the air scented with a strange mixture of sea salt and wild roses.

They were lazy days of soporific solitude only occasionally disturbed by a pack of screeching children in fluorescent swimming costumes.

In the evenings, Elizabeth cooked pasta with fresh ginger and yoghurt and we drank champagne with strawberries on the deck, as I explained the varying merits of television shows such as *The Bold and the Beautiful*, *The Young and the Restless* and, my then favourite, *General Hospital*. But one of my most vivid memories is of speeding down country lanes in Elizabeth's dark-blue Honda Prelude past salt marshes, long stretches of beach and woodland.

We stopped off to wander around picturesque villages and towns, such as Falmouth with its old sea captains' houses and craft shops, and Sandwich, the oldest settlement on Cape Cod.

Dating back to the Pilgrim traders of the early 17th century, Sandwich has a picture-perfect village green, a white church with steeple and is overflowing with pretty colonial houses, many of which are now B&Bs and antiques shops. Searching through the local art galleries, we bought a watercolour of a Cape Cod seascape for a friend who was getting married in Ohio later that summer.

One grey, blustery day we took a ferry across to Martha's Vineyard. I expected exclusive and was greeted with tacky. As we arrived in Oaks Bluff after a rough crossing, feeling decidedly queasy, a light drizzle fell on the brightly coloured gingerbread houses. The waterfront was a mass of hotels, souvenir shops and bars. We consumed vast quantities of seafood in a mock spit'n'sawdust bar as we sheltered from the rain. Martha's Vineyard may not have lived up to my expectations, but another day trip far exceeded them. Catching a Plymouth & Brockton bus to Boston I fell in love.

San Francisco had had an almost surreal magic and New York a frenetic buzz, but Boston felt like coming home. Stumbling upon the sign for the Cheers bar, I crept down the steps and lived another fantasy.

I had gone to the Cape to catch my breath. It was a stepping stone back to Europe, a whistle stop on the way. My memories are of a place full of light and water and wood and the greenest greens. Thinking of all I was leaving behind and all I was going back to, I wrote in my diary that I had even enjoyed the sour cream and onion chips, Haagen Dazs (I never did get into Ben and Jerry's) and Oprah.

On 1 September 1990, the first direct flights began between London Stansted and Havana. Within a decade, the number of British travellers to Cuba each year had risen from 1,200 to 100,000.

SOUTH LONDON TURNED INTO SRI LANKA, 1991

Fi Glover describes the surprising aftermath of a party in Clapham: a cricket match on a remote beach somewhere near Colombo.

You could hear the clamour of the taxi drivers back in passport control, and by the time you had come through baggage reclaim (a loose description) your face would be contorted into a rendition of Munch's *Scream* as you prepared to turn down the offers to ride in every Sri Lankan cab that met the big plane from London at Colombo airport.

Not me, though.

'Friend of Max's . . . friend of Max's?' asked the polite young man who came towards me as I crouched over my map of Sri Lanka. He could see that this was no ordinary, or sensible, map. It was, in fact, a photocopy on the back of a party invitation. As most maps should be. I had arrived in the still heat of Colombo equipped only with the following address: Max, Marrissa Beach, Sri Lanka.

And it really was written on the back of a party invitation. I can't remember now what the party itself was like, but since it was held in the early 90s I should think it entailed cheap wine, expensive king-size Rizlas, ludicrously strong cocktails and rather weak men. Its glamour lay in the fact that Max (the host) was going off to Harvard to do something with his big brain for a year and, between leaving Clapham and arriving in Boston, he was going to Sri Lanka for the summer. He wanted all his friends to join him. So the invitations had that photocopy on the back, with a little dot showing where Marrissa Beach was. And it just said 'come over'. I did.

So there's this lovely Sinhalese man at the airport and among all the clamour he's asking me whether I'm a friend of Max. So, of course, I say: 'Yes – why, do you know him too?' He says that he's in charge of some of the taxis, and that Max asked him to look out for pale young English people arriving on flights from London and point them in the right direction – southwest-ish. Fleeting thought: murderous, sweet-smiling serial killer, who says this to all the girls. But my mouth forms the reply: 'Lovely, yup. He's in Marrissa, isn't he? Can I get a cab there? Super, marvellous. Yes, thank you very much, how kind.'

The cab driver is equally lovely, and so we set off in a car that pays homage to a gearbox but doesn't appear to have one. If you take a cab out of Colombo and head south you soon lose the city, and the road follows the coast running between the white sands and the train line. Sometimes you go faster than the train; often you don't. It depends whether you're approaching a chicane of buffalo.

Five hours later we arrive in Marrissa. Now, I had thought on the way down that it might be a problem finding one tall, funny British bloke in what sounded like one of Sri Lanka's finest beach resorts. I was wrong. Marrissa Beach is just a beach, and back then Damarka's house and beach huts were the only accommodation available to optimistic Londoners. So we simply drove up to the gate, asked for Damarka, said hello, and at the mere mention of the name Max, realised that we had come to the right place. The taxi driver came in for dinner, and I walked out on to the beach to find that the party from Clapham had been pretty much transported in its entirety to a perfectly formed hut, surrounded by palms, with the sun dipping down over a low sea. So it was slightly better than Clapham, really.

Damarka turned out to be a star. He was a tiny Sinhalese with almost ebony skin and the cheekiest grin, and dancing eyes that were kept constantly amused by the stream of white faces arriving at his gate. The bloke back at the airport must have been busy.

We had a rather magical time at Marrissa Beach. Damarka built us another hut when the numbers swelled and he organised a cricket match when we hit twelve. We went down to the city of Galle to get a trophy made, and we played the local team on their pitch next door to Damarka's place. Guess what – we didn't get to keep the trophy. We girls were useless and kept trying to field in the shade, and we had to take a long tea break to get the water buffalo off the boundaries. The residents of Marrissa laughed a lot.

Max and the rest of the British cricket tour spent the whole of their summer there, but I had to return to my job filing bits of newspapers in a dungeon at the BBC. I wished I could have stayed longer. The only bad thing about the experience was that it made me keen to go to parties in Clapham. But maybe I'm being unfair. Maybe every Clapham cloud should have a Sri Lankan lining.

In 1991, Sri Lanka was five years into a vicious civil war that was to drag on for a further 10 years. The catalyst for a truce between government forces and the Liberation Tigers of Tamil Eelam was arguably an attack on Colombo airport that destroyed half the Sri Lankan airlines fleet.

TURNIN' INJUN, 1992

How Paul Copperwaite stopped worrying and learned to love America.

By the turn of the 1990s, I hadn't travelled much beyond the family holidays I had been too mature to go on for some time, and was not yet mature enough to go on again, and the odd lads' weekend in Amsterdam. I'd had a year off between school and college but it hadn't been a deliberate 'gap' year complete with cagoules, condoms and guidebooks. Instead, typically, it was the result of a paralysis of choice that meant I hadn't applied for university in time. Consequently I spent my year filling cartons in a shoe warehouse, and scraping a trowel across mottled earth, divining 13th-century toilet habits on a rain-drenched archaeological dig.

You'd have seen my pimply face then, callow and topped with a fifth-columnist's black woolly hat, on a CND demonstration, just one among thousands tramping on the grease-shined streets of central London. Cruise missiles rolled on flat-beds through the flat lands of my native East Anglia. Rumours in provincial pubs, as hushed as any uttered in Elizabethan coffee shops must have been, and loved in the telling like a modern ghost story, spoke of their night journeys. (They were probably hushed, of course, not in fear of some secret police, but in case they were overheard and corrected by someone who actually knew better.) In every prosaic, shaky shift towards consumerism that British culture made, I saw the dread threat of Americanisation.

Small wonder, then, that I would become connected by the strongest of ties to California, the biggest exporter of America to the states of the Union and, beyond it, the world. I fell in love with a Californian, and followed her home for the summer of 1992. This wasn't travel; this was life. After a monosyllabic, sun-blinded grilling by the Immigration and Naturalisation Service on account of my lack of a return ticket, we slumped for hours in our McMotel room, watching a desperate man in a pick-up in a real-time chase from which it was obvious there could be no escape. The continuity announcer helpfully told us, out of incoherent excitement rather than an empiricist's rigour, that the man was brandishing a 'silver-lookin' gun', and my snobby prejudices about the literacy and excitability of Americans were briefly confirmed.

Nonetheless my first trip to the West Coast confounded my expectations of *Baywatch* babes, buff boys and ripple-fleshed retirees. For a start, I spent the best part of a year in the leafy, temperate north, either the San Francisco Bay Area, the Central Valley, or in the tree-bearded top of the state amid giant sequoias, the oldest living things on the planet. As you drive from LA to the Bay Area, the light changes from the desert sun that bleaches the south and throws an architecture of shadows over every street, to the softer, flashing sun of the north of the state. Twisting and turning along Highway One, forest to the right and breakers to the left, I felt like I was in a 1980s tyre commercial. Twice the size of Cornish coves, so many beautiful beach vistas appeared at every turn that it's a wonder we arrived in one piece, it was so hard to keep my eyes on the road. On highways, it was hard too to stop changing lanes. The idea that you cruised where you were and it just sort of worked was a puzzle to my hierarchical British mind.

I'm sure my mother-in-law rejoiced as little in being a mother-in-law as I did in having one, but for my girlfriend and I to be together we'd tied the knot, against the fashion though it felt, so she was a worthwhile acquisition. Americans have to have a specific motive to be rid of you not to be hospitable, otherwise it's a compulsion they have, and my mom-in-law was no exception. Her kitchen was a homage to the commercial designer's art, with all manner of cans, packets and E-numbers. Re-creating it now in a Spitalfields gallery could be passed off as a homage to Warhol, and if it were found after an apocalypse by archaeologists, it would probably still be edible. I had a few culinary mishaps in even so English-speaking and self-publicised a place as California. I wouldn't, for example, recommend eating raw the white-trash shrink-wrapped sausage that looks like luncheon meat – the least porcine pork product I've ever come across and one which is meant to be fried – unless you're desperate for a very good excuse not to go out for a few days. Serves me right, I suppose, for buying it in the first place.

I couldn't be blamed, however, for drinking the tiny household ants, which are smaller than in the UK and which, when they get into the sugar and accrete themselves to the side of your cup of tea, look just like tiny tea leaves. As I recall, discovering I'd been doing this for a matter of weeks was more of a bombshell than nearly getting carjacked, if only because the latter happened with enough speed that it was as if I were someone else.

That, like the sausage episode, I brought on myself, a white rubbernecker alone in East Oakland, a gangsta rap capital in 1992, in his obliging mom-in-law's people carrier. I'd stopped at a crossing one evening. Three lads were gangbanging on the corner. Their eyes, like gun slits in pillboxes, drew a bead on me. In a second they were walking inscrutably towards the van, until one began to pull yet another silver-lookin' gun. It looked to be some kind of machine pistol since the clip was in front of the trigger. I didn't wait to see the tip of the barrel as I floored the pedal and hauled the van through the red light, braced for a crash that didn't come. On the rest of the journey I was invincible, and each time my heart rate slowed I became a little more American.

But the area had also been the wellspring of Beats and Hippies, home to Leary's proselytising and, not far away, to the Burning Man Festival, a desert Glastonbury where the people are the music, if you like. We hung with the Deadheads, my hippie chick and me, who dwelled full-time in old school buses, preferably purple, mirrored and velveteen, with split-screen VW vans for the weekenders, the slower the better. Fortunately they had less to do with the Grateful Dead than the name suggests. We parked up with them at Wavy Gravy's Hog Farm near Mendocino, where the smell of eucalyptus bathed your nostrils and the sun measured the day with a cooler–warmer–cooler routine that was predictable and perfect. Gone was the woolly hat of the fifth columnist in favour of a sun-kissed brow.

Wizardly men loped around Wavy's campsite, incanting 'buds for sale' like Chaucerian tradesmen. This was a million miles from the high-school hardship of American youth culture, in which the sports jocks and cheerleaders still held court like it was the 1950s. Now I swapped transatlantic notes on the warbling sibilances of folk-rock. I listened to recycled stories of noble native peoples, in which like was never compared with like: their spiritual and cultural beliefs with the conquering settlers' martial ruthlessness. I wondered if those impressions would have been so idealised had the outcome been different and the settlers' destiny in the Old West not so manifest. These were myths, like so many, of a time older and wiser than ours, which at least provided something to aspire to other than money.

Try as hard as I might to reassure myself with an Englishman's irony, I couldn't – I got it. I left at least some of my ego near San Francisco, and reflected on what a provincial, generalising prig I'd been in my anti-American views. The landscape had taken me in its hand, just as it had those toothless guys in felt pointy hats wandering among the sequoias, or the naked, mud-caked and anonymous bodies that were rolling around on the banks of the Eel River. I was at home in its oblivion, welcomed, not scared, by its space. I felt that life was more than it usually seemed to be, and that if I respected it, it would be kind to me. Oh God, I thought, I'll be buying whale-song CDs next.

We met The Mudman, naked and yet so caked in mud from the nearby riverbank that he was decent enough for tea at Browns', if without a tie. Only the whites of his eyes were distinguishable, along with his unfeasibly wide smile. I'd love to say he told us of mysteries gleaned from a troglodytic, mud-clad life on the land, but he didn't. He was an IT programmer from San Jose, just about to be swept up in the nascent dotcom bubble. Lying naked in the kaleidoscopic rays of the California sun, we extolled the state's virtues. He wouldn't have been able to stand the climate of northern Europe, he thought. I tried to explain the wintry pleasure to be had by a roaring hostelry fire, in a rollneck sweater, warming a single malt in your hands. Idealised, I know, but I was trying to make even a losing case. He fixed me with the stare of a greybeard loon, and planted an idea in my head. 'Next time you're doing that,' he said, 'you'll think of me.'

That was an innocent summer, after the Berlin Wall had come down and long before the same happened to the Twin Towers. Now I spare a thought for Americans, the blue-collar Jane and Joe, when I see them in London, ingenuous, bewildered and tired by the European creed of Inconvenience. Unprepared, they're fleeced for a pottery bobby or a teddy bear in a Union-flag waistcoat, blowing their fourteen-day annual holiday allowance if they're lucky. The vastness and grind of the USA gives few clues as to the ways in which the rest of the world differs, and meanwhile their intentions are good. And I still have some Californian values: peace of mind, an easy life, and to get by in the most comfortable way you can. Here's to you, Mudman!

On 16 September 1992, sterling lost one-quarter of its value against the dollar, when it spun out of the Exchange Rate Mechanism.

FRENCH EXCHANGE, 1992

Tim Wild recalls a teenage summer in Auxerre spent longing for the rolling hills of Wherevershire and cricket.

It was, to all intents and purposes, the first time that I had travelled abroad alone. No matter that I was literally put on the train by my French teacher and parents – and met at the other end by someone else's – throughout the journey from London's Victoria Station to the Burgundy region I imagined myself to be quite the cool loner. It was June 1992 – my hair was long, my jeans scuffed, and my guitar was slung casually over a shoulder, lending me in my imagination the air of someone with tales to tell and distance to travel. When I walked into the lobby of Auxerre train station, the looks on the faces of my hosts made it clear they fervently wished me to continue the journey, preferably for many miles.

My counterpart in this linguistic exercise, presumably chosen by some well-meaning dolt at the exchange agency, has a name that escapes me, so we'll call him Olivier. In fact, it's not just his name that escapes me, but his face, height, demeanour, and every other distinguishing characteristic. It's not my memory failing me now, though – they actually escaped me at the time. Perhaps it was just revenge for the many puerile jokes at my teacher's expense that term, but it seemed I was destined to spend the lion's share of a glorious summer with the most nondescript teenager in all France. This was made clear to me on the morning of day one, when I was forced to accompany Olivier to his school. The playground was full of kids, including many attractive girls, and my stumbling linguistic terror was mediated by the thought of at least getting to speak to some of these exotic goddesses, or smoke a fag or two with the hooded-top crew in the corner.

Fat chance. No one spoke to Olivier all day, the poor sod. In fact, people went out of their way not to do it, and in the rare moments I was alone and people spoke to me, they immediately melted away when they realised who'd brought me. His one companion, a small rat-faced individual, was equally unpopular. They had no doubt been forced into friendship by the harsh social dynamics of adolescence, and so terrified was he of being usurped by the foreign arrival that he wouldn't talk to me either. What fun I was going to have.

I would love to say that over the weeks, despite our lack of a shared language, I (accompanied by the strains of inspirational rock music) showed Olivier a thing or two about being fourteen, was myself slightly humbled, and that we high-fived our way to lifelong friendship. Instead, with the tact and sensitivity for which middle-class teenage boys are famous, I immediately and permanently shunned him, avoiding all but the most essential conversation, burying my head in the NME and mournfully plucking at my guitar.

When not at his school, I was at his house on Auxerre's outskirts, miles from the centre of town and surrounded by the flat and disappointing arable landscape that blights much of rural France. It actually wouldn't have made any difference if the poor bugger had lived in Cap d'Antibes, as Olivier's hideous parents would not have let him out anyway. After doing his homework as soon as he got home (I avoided mine) he and his doughy parents would religiously take their seats for the nightly lottery numbers, the sole familial activity to produce anything like levity. After that, they went to bed. This in a country where I could legally drink, in a season where it didn't get dark until 10 p.m. and where local girls (as I had been confidentially informed by a classmate) liked nothing better than to be bought a drink and wildly ravished in the nearest hedge. Needless to say, I felt very sorry for myself and determined, in the peculiar masochism of adolescence, to have absolutely the worst possible time.

At one point his mother tried to engage me in family life by indicating, with a mixture of hand gestures and a picture in a magazine, that she wanted me to play my guitar for the family. (I'd been clutching the thing to me like some sort of talisman since my arrival, convinced of its power to ward off the mundanity of my surroundings.) Barely had I reached the end of an excruciating rendition of 'You've Got To Hide Your Love Away' before my audience, without any smiles or applause, simply asked me to stop. There would be no more bridge-building attempts from either side.

After three days, I was practically gnawing my own limbs off. I'd played Olivier's Sega console till my eyes bled (a rare moment of digital understanding between us), and my dog-eared copy of the *NME* had been read so many times that I could recite whole articles from memory. At one point, hiding from the family in my room on a glorious sunny day, an English-language film came on the TV. It was about a village cricket team who are torn apart by World War II, and the kind of thing I'd normally have had eye surgery to avoid watching. But, as the rolling hills of Wherevershire filled the screen in black-and-white glory, and a very English chap asked someone about sandwiches in a clipped British accent, I cried and cried and cried.

There were, however, plans afoot to rescue me from my homesickness. In retrospect, I don't blame the poor woman – it must have been bad enough having one's own teenager sulking round the house making unpleasant smells and eating everything. Having an imported one whose very appearance flouted everything she believed in, who was stinking the place out, and scowling at everyone to boot, must have been intolerable. This did not in any way temper my shock and outrage, however, when one evening the phone rang (a rare enough occurrence in the Olivier household to be an event) and, following a flurried French conversation, my door opened and Olivier's mother handed me the receiver. 'Hello, is that Tim?' said a polite English voice. I expected disaster, some terrible news about the family at home whom I'd come to idolise over the last three days. 'Olivier's mother has decided that things aren't working out and she wants you to leave. We've found another family for you – we'll pick you up tomorrow morning.'

Well, honestly. Despite the fact I'd seriously considered climbing out of the window and running off into the night several times, the realisation that the witch-faced cow had the impudence to want me off her premises was deeply infuriating. 'It's your fault, you know,' I wanted to shout, pointing at Olivier. 'He'll do everything he's told until his mid-twenties and then start wearing women's pants or coldly murder all his colleagues in the tax office or something, and all your purse-lipped moral rectitude will have been for nothing!' I instead said very little except a meek thank you, and got into the car like I was told.

As it turned out, it was the best thing for everyone, especially me. I was shipped off to a new family down the road who had, among other things, a blonde, seventeen-year-old daughter who thought my 'air was vereee cute', an exchange partner whose mates immediately taught me any number of unmentionable French phrases and took me off to vandalise the railway, and, best of all, another English exchange student called Zeta (partnered with the sister) whose enthusiasm for afternoons getting plastered in French taverns matched mine glass for cheap glass. The peculiar thing was that, despite me having another Brit for company, I actually started to learn something. The enthusiasm and kindness the family showed me was heart-warming. They kindly insisted on French in their presence, and since they were so nice, I wanted to hang out with them all the time. After two weeks of doing everything from attending lavish, four-hour dinners with their friends and neighbours to attempting to teach their two-year-old 'Hotel California' in French, I was thinking in French, actually enjoying unsalted butter, and shrugging indifferently with the best of them. Not only did I accidentally enjoy some of the best times of my life, but also, against almost all expectations, passed my GCSE French with such dexterity that during my oral exam, I was asked to slow down because my fluency wouldn't be heard properly on tape. So, Olivier, if you're out there, I really hope you told your parents to stuff it and began to enjoy yourself. If not, please don't murder all your colleagues, OK?

On 7 July 1992, *Eldorado*, a BBC soap opera set among a British expatriate community in southern Spain, began transmission. It was a huge flop, and was canned within a year.

WHAT AM I DOING HERE? 1993

A journey to Patagonia spelled the end of Rhiannon Batten's love affair with travel literature.

It was January 1993, the middle of the summer in Chile. The old woman who had snored along to the train's night-time soundtrack of clanking and whistling had got off at the last stop and yesterday's view of endless dusty fields had been replaced with dewy pastures and ancient, skewwhiff houses. As the train pulled in to Puerto Montt, halfway down the country, I skipped on to the platform as fast as my obese rucksack allowed and took the first steps on my gap-year journey to Patagonia.

A few months before, I'd been stuck in the Welsh borders, studying for A-levels. Bruce Chatwin's story of his search for the remains of the giant South American sloth, *In Patagonia*, had been my excuse for a bit of revision avoidance. It was geography, wasn't it, I fooled myself, flicking from page to page while ignoring the fact that my looming geography exam would be focusing more on the logistics of Brasilia's business district than kinship patterns in the pampas.

Crucial though a sketchy knowledge of South America's town planning was likely to be, Chatwin's tales of immigrant Argentinians called Gwynneth and Euan, who preferred their lamb pepped up with chilli and garlic but liked nothing better than whiling away their days with a few Wesleyan hymns at the local chapel, made much more compulsive reading. Even if, as critics later suggested, Chatwin had misrepresented many of the people he'd met.

This was familiar territory. Growing up abroad, my Welsh father had instilled a sense of cultural history in my sister and

I by sending us to school on St David's Day sprouting a crop of plastic daffodils and leeks on our chests, pinned to the Welsh wench costumes that had been devotedly knitted for us by our grandmother back in Swansea. In his book, Chatwin describes this devotion to keeping the Welsh culture alive as 'the authentic, blinkered passion of the exile'. But, for the travel-obsessed, it is also what adds the quirk that makes a destination stand out from the more easily categorised crowd.

So, when I failed to get into my first-choice university and was told to try again the following year (when I'd done more reading), I saw it as a chance to visit some of the places Chatwin had written about. Saving up the money I'd earned flogging Levellers CDs in the local WH Smith, I eventually had enough for a plane ticket – and a glossy new copy of *South America on a Shoestring* – and set off to Santiago, in Chile, on New Year's Eve 1992. There may be closer airports to Patagonia, but my mother's friend Susan lived in Santiago and Mum had decided I'd be safer staying with her, even if it limited my South American explorations to sipping *café cortado* in the Plaza de Armas in the Chilean capital. An unwise move, given that Susan had spent the last twenty years travelling around South America. When I told her my plans, she helpfully drove me to the station and put me on the next train south, to Puerto Montt.

Determined to follow in Chatwin's footsteps, I took a three-day bus through Argentina to Punta Arenas with four friendly Chilean girls I'd met in a youth hostel. The next town from here, a bleak and wind-scuffed place almost at the very tip of South America, was Puerto Natales. This was the last stop before the cave where Chatwin's search had ended, and the point where I had intended my own trip to really begin.

It didn't quite turn out that way. En route to Puerto Natales I met Michael, a backpacker and wannabe squaddie from North Wales. He was planning a five-day trek around the granite towers, thick forests and frozen ice fields of Torres del Paine National Park and wanted me to go with him. Given my lack of experience, camping equipment and, more worryingly, conviction that this was someone I wanted to be alone with in a 240,000-acre wilderness, I did the only sensible thing for an impressionable girl with an obsession for all things Welsh. I agreed. Three days later, having been marched through the rain at break-leg speed, propelled bottom-first towards a glacier, made to sleep in a giant plastic bag (the closest substitute for canvas Puerto Natales had offered), I was close to despair. It wasn't the physical hardship that had got me. It was being forced to listen to Michael's steamrollering sentimentality about his homeland: the tributes to his granny's Welsh cakes, his encyclopedic knowledge of the part played by the Welsh regiments in the Second World War, the lamentations about the form of Cardiff City.

Finally, a late-night rendition of 'Bread of Heaven', delivered over a plate of half-eaten spaghetti, broke me. The next morning I took the first bus back to Santiago, my expatriate's rose-tinted vision gone forever. At the end of the week, it was time to go home. Before driving me to the airport Susan suggested one final jaunt. I feared the worst when she said it was 'literary', but the poet Pablo Neruda's house at Isla Negra turned out to be one of the highlights of my trip. *Hasta la vista*, Bruce, I thought. Next time I'd exercise my love affair with a travel writer with a little more care.

At the start of 2004, many trains in Chile were suspended pending what was said to be improvement work on the line. Some were due to start running in December 2004.

EVEN THE FISH WERE DRESSED FOR FOOTBALL, 1994

Matthew Cole goes football crazy in Roatan. Just don't mention the Worldcup.

Italy's Roberto Baggio stepped up to the penalty spot. I could barely look. But the Brazilians sensed this was their moment. They stared at him, then at me. I tried not to catch their eye, silently willing Baggio on.

In the Californian heat of Pasadena's Rose Bowl stadium, Baggio began his run-up. Several thousand miles south down the Pan American highway in a resort compound on the Honduran island of Roatan, the Brazilians ignored the tropical sunshine outside and stared even harder at the TV set.

I stared at the floor. Thud. I looked up, and my heart sank. No bulging net, no Italian celebrations. The ball had gone high over the bar and Brazil had won the World Cup.

The tanned young Brazilians around me tipped back their heads and howled with delight. Lost in the middle of their carnival, I was now as invisible to them as the miserable Baggio was to the ecstatic Brazilian team on the pitch. The barman cranked up the stereo and Baggio wandered off, head in hands. I could not pretend to have been supporting Brazil all along, any more than he could have switched teams.

Inaudible above the chants of 'Bra-sil! Bra-sil!' it is a safe bet that the TV commentator was describing Baggio as the loneliest man in the world. I knew how he felt. As scrums of holidaying fans teetered playfully towards the pool I headed back to the beach feeling strangely homesick and wondering why I had done it again.

* * *

USA 94 was not the first World Cup I had made the mistake of watching while far from the safety of home. Four years earlier the venue had been a back-street bar in an Andean market town in Ecuador. The final act of Italia 90 was being played out in Rome, between the white man, or gringo, and the whole of South America. Well, at least that is how the handful of villagers who glared at me as West Germany beat Argentina one–nil seemed to look at it.

It is not that the people of Ecuador or Honduras were ever really hostile. Or that I am an ungracious traveller. The problem, as David Beckham can confirm, is that football dredges up some horribly inappropriate responses. And they are best left to the privacy of your own home country.

It is too personal. And you cannot explain things: like the way those Ecuadoreans saw the Argentine team as South American crusaders pitted against an evil gringo enemy represented by the West German team, my girlfriend and me. Or why walking into a holiday resort packed with the families of Brazil's wealthiest industrialists led me to support the vain European cause against the world's mightiest football machine.

Only after the final whistle can you come to your senses. Just two hours after finding myself an Italy fan for the first time in my life, football could not have been further from my mind.

I was on the white sands of West End, Roatan, shopping for a diving course at the dive shops up and down the beach of Half Moon Bay. Roatan is one of the 'Bay Islands' off Honduras's Caribbean coast and one of the cheapest and best scuba resorts in the world. While Brits tend to go to Belize, this is where the Americans come – along with a few Brazilians.

Over the next two weeks of gawping at a fantasia of undersea flora and fauna, there were few reminders of football. Like most of his compatriots, our American diver-master was more interested in spotting barracuda, manta ray and the beautiful lace-finned drumfish around the reef than discussing the 'Worldcup' – he and his kind pronounced it as one word, like teacup. You see, even that was annoying.

I was doing well at putting it to the back of my mind, though I could not help recognising the team strips of the squads of tropical fish flitting in formation across the coral. And I am not sure whether the flashy Brazil-supporting angelfish were not significantly outplayed by the classier royal blue brilliance of the guppies.

While the Brazilians and I could not forget its real significance, on Roatan the World Cup was a novelty. This is an island whose black Garifuna population has a completely separate culture from that of the Spanish-speaking mainland. Roatan natives speak an English-based Caribbean patois and youth culture in the big 'city' capital of Coxen Hole is dominated by Jamaican ragga and American baseball.

Ecuador, of course, is a different story. For the Spanish Mestizo population, if not the indigenous Andeans, football is big bananas – though in Ecuador nothing is quite as big as bananas. I watched Germany beating Argentina in the market town of Otovalo, a place famous for the enterprise of its native population. Its massive market has made it such a popular stop on the backpacker circuit that you feel it is only a matter of time before there is a Hard Rock Café on the high street. For years there has been a pudding shop where blackberry and apple pies are served by the square yard, with ice cream or custard.

But there is no TV in the pudding shop. Eventually we found a bar with a TV set and stepped out of the beautiful Andean daylight into the dark, candlelit bar to squint at a cathode-ray snowstorm through which you could just make out an impression of a match. I wished we had not bothered. Yet it is now my favourite story. Maybe there was, after all, some bond we shared with our fellow football fans in that bar. They knew that, like them, we were fans. And that meant that for a split second we knew exactly how much they hated us. If there is one certainty about a World Cup final, it is that the commentator at one stage will refer to the millions watching all round the world.

When that happens, spare a thought for the Brit abroad, about to have a perfectly good holiday ruined.

On 14 November 1994, the first scheduled Eurostar train departed from London Waterloo to Paris at 8.23 a.m.

EVEN BEARS HAVE BAD BREATH, 1995

She'd planned a trip to the Russia's Altai mountains and Lake Teletskoye – but Margaret Campbell hadn't planned for such close encounters with dangerous animals.

'Phoo, Misha, phoo!' The usual Russian response to irksome animals wasn't working: Misha, a three-month-old bear, and looking as cuddly as any self-respecting roly-poly brown cub should (but with a bad case of halitosis), kept trying to play and her cute paws hid some sharp claws. When Svetlana had suggested organising a back-to-nature journey to the Altai mountains in lieu of payment for translation work with her science journal, I hadn't bargained on getting quite so close to Russia's wildlife.

Misha notwithstanding, the trip to the Altai was one of the highlights of a two-year stay in Siberia. Our initial two soon grew to a convivial six, as everyone in the Novosibirsk-based editing team decided that this was too good an opportunity to pass up. We were promised basic, free accommodation at a research station by Lake Teletskoye.

Tatyana cooked enough food to last her husband and children through a siege, Natasha pleaded with her daughter not to give birth for another couple of weeks, Denis brought along his wife and, leaving the cares of the city behind us, we headed off, bumping along on the floor of an ex-army truck now used as a mobile laboratory.

The journey took the better part of a day: three and a half hours south to Barnaul, then a few more hours through Biysk and upwards into the Gorno Altai Autonomous Republic. It wasn't far from the border to our destination, the village of Artybash, but the road surface was dreadful, and it was dark when we arrived.

We woke to blazing sunshine and the shimmering surface of Lake Teletskoye, shaped rather like an upside-down Italy. A group of Belgian geologists were also at the base, examining rock formations along the shoreline: two of them had cadged a lift in our truck from Novosibirsk and returned the favour by letting us join them on a two-day trip.

Such co-operation would once have been impossible in this remote corner, where the Russian, Kazakhstan, Chinese and Mongolian borders meet, but times had changed.

The lake is fed from mountain streams and remains virtually unpolluted (I was surprised at first to see the scientists happily brushing their teeth in it). We stopped off several times while the geologists took rock samples and we explored sights such as Korba waterfall. In the evening the men camped near the mouth of the Chulyshman river, providing the local mosquitoes with rich pickings, while we women tried to find refuge on the boat. After a fireside picnic on the first night, Katya and Svetlana sang Russian songs, the geologists responded with Jacques Brel, and it fell to me to show what Scotland could come up with (an off-key rendition of 'The Skye Boat Song' and 'Flower of Scotland').

The next day we came across three game wardens who had just spent forty days walking and riding through the huge nature reserve along the eastern shore of the lake, on the lookout for poachers. After the first few days they had survived on what they could find or trap but, apart from ravenous hunger (I've never seen a tin of condensed milk go down quite so fast), they seemed none the worse for wear.

* * *

Back at the base, we were reminded of the need for such men when someone brought in a bear cub, left behind when poachers had killed its mother for her skin.

Misha was being temporarily fed and sheltered by the scientists, but unless they could find her a new home in a zoo or circus, she would have to be shot; she would soon be too dangerous to keep at the base, but incapable of surviving in the wild.

We stayed for another week in Artybash, watching hundreds of white and purple butterflies startle up from the ground as we passed, swimming in mountain streams and enjoying some rest. The men carried water up from the lake so that we could use the *banya* (the Russian sauna) and we cooked and ate in the open air, and drank toasts to everybody and everything imaginable.

On our return journey, we spent a night sleeping outside by the powerful Katun river, mosquito-free; our first rainy afternoon, wandering through Gorno-Altaysk waiting for the truck to be repaired; and enjoying hospitality with friends of Svetlana in Biysk: all too soon, we were back outside the publisher's office, and I left for Moscow two days later.

I returned to Novosibirsk in 1999. Sadly there was no time to travel to the Altai, but we sat round Svetlana's table and took stock: finances for the English-language journal have dried up, but Svetlana finally has a suitable flat and Katya is married to an Australian she met through the Internet. Natasha has a four-year-old grandson, Denis is an awestruck father – and Misha has found a home in Novosibirsk's recently upgraded zoo.

On 10 November 1995, a Greek-Cypriot shipping millionaire named Stelios Haji-Iaonnou launched easyJet's first flight, from Luton to Glasgow. The aircraft and crew were hired from a BA affiliate, GB Airways. Passengers paid a fare of £29.

TROUBLE IN PARADISE, 2002

The promise to 'Be your own Robinson Crusoe' didn't turn out quite as planned, as James Marriott discovered at the end of his summer sojourn in Central America.

It had been a good summer so far. I'd made it to thirty, had my first book published, and had been enjoying a long and entirely undeserved break in Central America. From impromptu meetings with Guatemalan witches to being almost lynched as a child snatcher in a remote mountain village, it had been an eventful trip. But the lure of the sea had now caught me, and I'd eschewed my bedbug budget in favour of some luxury dive sites off Honduras and Belize. But the islands I'd been on had shops, restaurants and other tourists; I knew there was more of an adventure out there – it was just a matter of finding it.

It was in a diner in Belize City, scoffing an unlikely plate of bacon and eggs, that I first saw the Sittee River ad. 'Be your own Robinson Crusoe,' it crowed. The place sounded idyllic: a remote island in a marine park, two hours from the Belize coast. No running water, no electricity, cook your own food, swim with the fishes.

But when I turned up at the Sittee River guesthouse to sign up for the trip, the Frenchman who greeted me seemed surprised. The island was normally closed to visitors from September to November, he told me, but it had been a slow year and they'd take whoever they could get now. If I wanted to swim in the river there, he advised me, I should stick close to the boat, as there were crocodiles; one had eaten a small dog just a few days before. He laughed as he told me this, which instantly endeared him to me, as I detest small dogs.

Later that day a Hungarian couple, Dora and Tibor, arrived, who would be my companions on the island retreat. I was happy to have someone else along – the minimum stay was a week, and there was no way to get off the island before then, other than chartering a boat for $250. They seemed pleasant enough, a young married couple hoping to frolic in the surf.

We were taken out to the island in a speedboat by an uncommunicative Belizean man and his American wife, Becky, who were accompanied by their three children, all with the blond hair and glittering blue eyes of a sanity long corroded through enforced isolation. This didn't prepare us for the sight of Becky's mother lumbering down the beach to meet us, her over-tanned and leathery hide falling in folds over her skimpy bikini, attached to the bottom of which were a few sheets of toilet paper gaily flapping in the wind. Becky pointed this out to her mother, who tucked them into her bikini bottoms and started on her tour of the island with us.

As she moved with elephantine grace down the sun-bleached coral paths, pointing out the garbage pit and communal kitchen, overrun with hermit crabs, some of which had eschewed the more traditional shell as their home in favour of jetsam from previous visitors, bottle caps and vitamin jars, I noticed that she would not make eye contact with any of us, her dull, affectless gaze fixed perpetually on the near distance. The time came for her to dispense snorkelling equipment, so I told her I had my own, and went off to swim around some of the reefs. Before I left she asked me if I dived. I told her I did.

'Do you want to go diving tomorrow morning?'

'Uh –'

'That's settled then, be here at around nine.'

I wasn't sure about this, as the diving on the island looked extremely expensive, around $80 a tank, but I was a little hung over and had allowed myself, as is usual in such a state, to be bullied into passivity.

When I returned from my snorkel, excited after having seen sleeping nurse sharks and eagle rays gliding through the water, I found Dora and Tibor cowering in the kitchen. They told me that the grandmother had bullied them into taking unsuitable snorkelling equipment, fins that didn't fit and leaky masks, and had insisted that the large-footed Tibor pay $10 a day extra for a pair of booties along with his fins. Shell-shocked, they had wandered away with this kit, then, their courage returning as they were away from the malign influence of the grandmother, they returned and gave all of the kit back, deaf to the protestations of the family that they would have a terrible time without it. This decided me: I wasn't going to do any diving here, and I walked off to the house, not without a degree of trepidation, to tell them.

As I approached, I wondered what I'd find – the family fishing together, or lolling in their hammocks reading. Perhaps their long isolation had led some of them to pursue eccentric and arcane pursuits, such as the construction of a worm observatory. But no. As I got closer I could hear shouting.

'You asshole! This is my kitchen!' Becky was screaming at her mother, as the children cowered in the corner. As the two women flung increasingly vicious obscenities at each other I asked the husband if I should come back later. He shrugged and asked me what I wanted.

'I don't think I'll be doing any diving here.'

'OK.'

This threw me, as I'd expected an argument, and I blustered on.

'It's because you – don't have a prescription mask. I can't really see much without one.'

'OK.' Fine.

As we cooked together that evening Tibor fantasised about how to escape if things went pear-shaped. There was another island nearby; perhaps we could swim there. We imagined the grandmother, her mind bent by decades of overexposure to the harsh tropical sun, snapping, scuttling the boats and murdering her family before lumbering after us. It was all too clear in our minds: 'No, Granny, don't!' The thud of the cleaver. The hiss of arterial spray. The low, throaty chuckle. The gore-soaked bikini. We camped near each other as an early-warning system, and found that evening that the island was plagued with mosquitoes as well as the sandflies endemic to these islands.

As the days went by, the diet of packet pasta and the wearing assault by insects began to take its toll. Too listless, finally, to swim, we would weakly swat at the insects or sit in the shallow water attempting feebly to peel coconuts. Full of adventure when I'd arrived, I'd bounded around the island barefoot only to gash the soles of both feet on the razor-sharp coral. The wounds quickly became ulcerated by constant contact with salt water, until walking was agony. The Hungarian couple had their own problems: Tibor had burned his lower lip in the sun, and it was starting to blister into a purulent mess. I sympathised, having suffered from the same affliction for a month earlier on: nothing heals in the tropics. He had also contracted an earache, and writhed around on the beach chairs like a salted slug, counting the minutes until he could be safely removed from the island. The already willowy Dora was becoming increasingly eti- olated, her eyes taking on a consumptive glitter quite at odds with her physical lethargy, like Olive Oyl with a thyroid deficiency. We started to hoard our food, eyeing each others' tuck with ill-disguised hunger and hatching elaborate plans to exchange biscuit for tea bag, stick of spaghetti for potato peel.

When we finally left, the rabid granny having been apparently moved off the island on an earlier boat, presumably despatched by Becky after a particularly intense argument, we asked the boat captain to stop at the first shop on the river banks on the mainland, where we chewed on stale Snickers bars and felt the beauty of the sugar rush.

I realised why the European resort worker I'd met in the Maldives had propped up the bar alone or with whoever he could get every night, courting oblivion: isolation, even – or especially – on a remote island 'paradise', led neither to a state of noble savagery, an 'at oneness' with nature, nor to an overflowing of the creative well, untrammelled by the urbanite's mediated information overload. My romantic image of a solo tranquillity, fuelled by a thousand murderous tube journeys, peeled away to reveal the yawning gulf beneath. I liked people, I realised; or maybe that wasn't it – many were impossibly irritating, after all. What I liked was . . . options. Enforced isolation was more solitary confinement mind-warp than idyllic palm frond: I was now ready to go home.

Contrary to my previous experiences on returning to the UK after a long sojourn abroad, this time it felt like the right place to be. Since then I've operated on the assumption that the exotic is a state of mind as much as of place, and found trips to North Wales as alien and bizarre as any cloud forest hike in the Guatemalan Highlands. But maybe that's just me.

In 2002, British Airways abandoned its main links serving Central America, dropping flights to both San Jose in Costa Rica and to Cancun in Mexico.